To Uncl
Lane ,

CH00602526

9?.. September 2004

JOHN BUNYAN
HIS LIFE and TIMES

Vivienne and Lewis Evans

Preface by Terry Waite
Foreword by The Bishop of Bedford

ELSTOW

The Abbey Church of St. Mary and St. Helena, Elstow

The
Book
Castle

To Canon Edward Charles
A Pilgrim for Peace

First published July 1988
by
The Book Castle
12 Church Street
Dunstable
Bedfordshire LU5 4RU

This slightly revised edition
published June 1995

Typeset by Avocet Marketing Services, Bicester, Oxon.
Revisions by Keyword, Aldbury, Herts.
Printed by Antony Rowe Ltd., Chippenham, Wilts.

ISBN 1 871199 87 5

Reprinted 1998

Reprinted May 2001

The cover pictures are details from a painting by A. Breanski, showing St. Cuthbert's Street before the cottages were demolished in 1838. (Courtesy: Bunyan Museum, Bedford).
Front cover: The gabled cottage was the home of John Bunyan and his family from the mid-1650s until his death in 1688. The small window gave a little light into 'Bunyan's parlour'; a bar of the grate was stamped J. B. The larger room, on the left, was the family living room; there was also a small study. In this cottage his two eldest sons were born, his first wife and eldest daughter died and his second wife gave birth to his two youngest children. Number 17 St. Cuthbert's Street bears a commemorative plaque.
Back cover: Only forty-seven families lived in St. Cuthbert's parish in 1660 when bunyan was prosecuted for refusing to take the Anglican form of communion at this parish church. Here, however, his son Joseph was baptised on November 12, 1672 and his daughter Sarah was married fourteen years later.

Preface

Never for one moment did I expect my name to become linked with that of the great John Bunyan. It happened because an ordinary resident of Bedford thought that a simple postcard might give me some hope while I languished in prison. It was the only mail I received during years of solitary confinement. This kindly act drew me to want to know more about Bedford's most famous son and Vivienne Evans' excellent book has been of help to me in my quest. It is most attractively written and produced and gives an excellent overview for the general reader.

In these pages the author gives an insight into how a man from a very ordinary background became known throughout the world. To understand the man it is necessary to understand the age in which he lived, and, in a few words, Mrs Evans paints a fascinating picture.

Since my release I have discovered something of the hidden treasures of Bedfordshire; Elstow and the Bunyan Museum being just two mentioned in this book. There are many more waiting to be found by visitors, who, if they will set out with this book will be able to make their own discoveries.

Terry Waite, Suffolk 1995

Visit of Terry Waite to the Moot Hall, Elstow, on 30 November, 1994. Watched by the Curator, Sally Myers, he is discussing with the author a feature on John Bunyan's Bedfordshire for BBC Radio's programme, Going Places, broadcast on Friday 20 January, 1995. (Photograph courtesy of Bedfordshire County Council.)

3

Terry Waite
and the
John Bunyan Postcard

It was in November 1991 that Archbishop Runcie's special envoy, Terry Waite, was released, after 1,763 days as a prisoner of Muslim extremists, in Beirut.

Immediately following his release, at a press conference filmed by television cameras from all over the world, he spoke of a picture postcard. This depicted John Bunyan writing 'The Pilgrim's Progress', during the long period that he had spent in prison during the 17th century.

Many letters and postcards had been sent to Terry Waite during the years that he had spent in solitary confinement but for various reasons none of them had even been delivered to his cell.

Then one day a card arrived from Mrs Joy Brodier, a young mother from Brickhill, near Bedford; it carried a simple message – 'We remember. We shall not forget. We shall continue to pray for you and and to work for all people who are detained around the world'.

The picture was a photograph of a stained glass window at the Bunyan Meeting Free Church, Mill Street, Bedford. It was purchased from money raised by public subscription in 1978, the 300th anniversary of the publication of 'The Pilgrim's Progress' and shows Bunyan in a prison cell with quill in hand.

Manacled to the wall and with no possible chance of recording his thoughts let alone writing books, Terry Waite had to rely on his memory. He told the reporters that although this card became a link with the outside world and gave him strength to look forward to the future and eventual return to home in England, it also made him compare his situation with that of Bunyan. He thought how lucky Bunyan had been to have his own clothes, a window through which he could see the world outside, and a pen and paper to mark down his thoughts.

Soon after his arrival back in England Terry Waite wrote to thank Mrs Brodier and promised to visit her as soon as possible and at the same time to see for himself the inspiring window.

Photograph courtesy of Bedfordshire County Council.

They later met at a service held at the Meeting House and Terry Waite became patron of an appeal, launched by leaders of the church, to raise £300,000 to refurbish the church and to relocate the Bunyan museum. The card, which has been reproduced as a greetings card, with the words 'Remembering You', has become a focal point of the appeal.

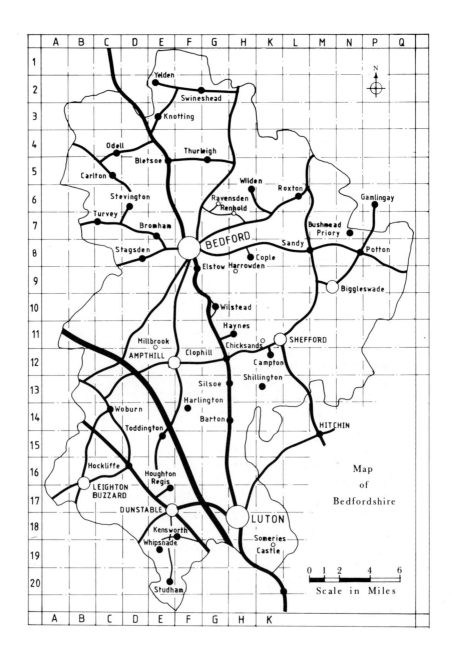

Map
of
Bedfordshire

Scale in Miles

0 1 2 4 6

Contents

Bunyan's statue, Bedford. The gift of Hastings, ninth Duke of Bedford, executed by J.E. Boehm. Erected in 1874 at the corner of St Peter's Green

Foreword

The Right Reverend David J. Farmbrough
The Bishop of Bedford (1981 to November 1993)

At the centre of Bedford town stands the statue of John Bunyan. I guess that few of those who regularly walk past that statue have much idea about the story of that distinguished man of Bedford and Bedfordshire. It is therefore particularly good in the tercentenary of his death to have published a book which puts John Bunyan into the context of the religious and social setting of the 17th century in Bedfordshire. This is the local story of a national figure who is increasingly becoming recognised and appreciated by every Christian tradition. I hope this story will send many of us back to read or read again Bunyan's spiritual masterpiece *The Pilgrim's Progress* and help us to appreciate that the Christian life is a pilgrimage of faith and hope towards that love which is at the heart of all things.

During a celebration held at the Bunyan Meeting Free Church, June 19 1988, to mark the 300th anniversary of Bunyan's death, the author gave Lord Runcie, the then Archbishop of Canterbury, a signed copy of the first edition of this book.

John Bunyan by Robert White. By kind permission of Bedfordshire County Council.

Authors' Introduction

1988 was the tercentenary of the death of John Bunyan, a man who was born in the county of Bedfordshire and who, apart from a short period during the Civil War, lived there throughout the 60 years of his life.

He wrote in total over 60 books and pamphlets in addition to his world famous, *The Pilgrim's Progress*. Although he came from a humble village background and had little formal education, it is calculated that over 100,000 copies of *The Pilgrim's Progress* in English were sold in his lifetime plus editions in seven other languages. It has now been translated into over 200 different languages and is a world best seller, second only to the Bible.

This present book does not set out to be a formal biography of John Bunyan but attempts to show his local background. The 17th century has been described as a 'century of change' and it was that combined social, political and above all religious upheaval which moulded the young man, led to his spiritual distress and his search for 'the peace' which he finally found in the love and forgiveness of his Lord Jesus Christ.

Several of his other and less well known works are also discussed in this book in an attempt to illustrate the conscientious, thoughtful and most appealing man who appears from between their covers.

As an author, Bunyan drew on his experiences as a country child, an itinerant traveller, a young soldier, a husband and father and above all as a pilgrim, who, like his 'hero' Christian, struggled to find his way along life's difficult road until he found the Celestial City.

The book ends with five appendices: Appendix I: The Bunyans of Elstow, the first attempt to produce in print an account of the Bunyan family history. Appendix II: a brief account of 17th century Elstow. Appendix III: some suggestions of 17th century features that can be visited in Bedfordshire today. Appendix IV: looks at sites in modern Bedfordshire with Bunyan connections. Appendix V: searches for the original sites featured in *The Pilgrim's Progress*.

Vivienne and Lewis Evans

Credits

Many people have helped us with the production of this book.

The staff at the County Record Office and County Libraries, in particular Mr Barry Stephenson for whose help and encouragement I have been especially grateful, and Miss Patricia Bell, who when reading through the manuscript made several suggestions to help clarify the complicated religious situation of the mid-17th century. I would, however, point out that the final interpretation is my own and I am entirely responsible for any mistakes which have occurred.

Numerous people have helped with the actual production but we would particularly like to thank Adèle Kane, Joyce Maxfield, Marlene Pothecary and G. E. M. Office Stationery, for their continual, willing and cheerful support. Also, Victoria Huxley who has given us the benefit of her professional skills as editor.

We would like to thank the many people who allowed us to take photographs or who lent us their own photographs and Mr Lee Stanley who processed them, often with only a few hours' notice.

Finally, we would like to thank Mr Paul Bowes, whose friendship, patience and unflagging support has made the whole thing possible.

Vivienne and Lewis Evans
March 1988

We are very pleased to acknowledge a grant from Aerospace Composite Technologies, Luton, towards the cost of reprinting this book (see p.224).

Vivienne and Lewis Evans
June 1995

CHAPTER ONE

The Bunyans of Bedfordshire

Bunyan Family Origins

John Brown* has suggested that the name 'Bunyan' is of Norman origin and that the family arrived in Bedfordshire as relatives of Nigel d'Albini, whose main family residence became Cainhoe Castle. This is backed up by the fact that recorded in the Annals of Dunstable Priory, sometime before 1219, is a family called 'Bunyun' who owned land in Pulloxhill, alongside land owned by the Albini family.

Whether or not these Bunyuns were connected with a Bunyan family living in Dunstable and the south Bedfordshire villages, or the Bunyans of Elstow and Bedford, we do not know. It is, however, recorded that as early as 1199 a 'William Buniun' was renting land at Wilstead (two miles from Harrowden) from the Abbess of Elstow.

The Bunyans of Elstow

In the 17th century the most popular christian names for the Elstow Bunyans are Thomas, John and William, and as early as 1327 we can identify a 'William Boynon' living at Harrowden with his wife Matilda.

The manor court rolls for Elstow have survived for the middle years of the 16th century. Amongst the freemen represented in 1542 was a 'Thomas Bonyon'. His father, also Thomas, had recently died and this Thomas had inherited the family house and adjoining paddock at Harrowden, plus nine acres of land in the common fields. In later

---

*Much of the information in this chapter was researched and published by John Brown in his biography *John Bunyan – His Life, Times and Work*.

Earthworks on site of Cainhoe Castle. H12

The cottage in which John Bunyan was born, date unknown. By kind permission of Bedfordshire County Council. G9

deeds, the position of these acres is described in relation to neighbouring strips, and can, with an estate map made in 1767 be reasonably well identified.

This Thomas is described as 'of the age of forty years and more' and in a later deed as 'labourer', but, as we shall see below, that description of employment is very general and does not necessarily represent poverty. A century later, the 'Thomas Bunyans', father and son, were respectively a chapman and a brazier.

A chapman was a salesman, who walked around the countryside with a pack of small domestic items, or possibly travelled with a donkey or a pony and cart. A brazier was a respected member of the community. He may have travelled around the countryside but took many jobs home to his own furnace. Tinkers were men who travelled across the country doing small metal repairs before moving on. Because of this they were often strangers and not trusted. John Bunyan referred to himself as a 'tinker'; this may be because, as a young man, he travelled around measuring up jobs for his father and doing small repairs on the spot, or because he had no furnace of his

An example of the work of a 17th-century brazier; Weathercock dated 1630.

own when he set up as a young married man.

During the next few years Thomas (Junior) sold off several acres of land but this does not necessarily mean that the family were suffering distress; it is quite likely that he wanted to invest his time and money into some more lucrative craft or business. He was a householder apparently respected in the community and was elected constable in 1547. It is also made clear in the court rolls that the family had some other business beside agriculture.

In an attempt to control the price of staple foods a maximum price was fixed each year for bread and beer. This was supposed to vary with the price of cereals, depending on the success or otherwise of the previous year's harvest. Although elected officials were supposed to keep a check on the quality of the finished products, the fixed maximum price did tend to encourage a weaker brew and some brewers were fined year after year at the manor court 'for breaking the assize', i.e. selling weak beer.

A century later John Bunyan writing about a 'penny loaf', pointed out:

> 'The price one penny is in time of plenty,
> In famine doubled, 'tis from one to twenty'.

During the 1550s, Thomas Bunyan or his wife were repeatedly fined for breaking the assize of both bread and beer and it appears that they must have kept a small inn which served both food and drink. This suggestion is backed up in 1554 by the description of this Bunyan, or another, as 'victualler'. The surviving manor court rolls end in 1550 but on 20 November 1554 some men from Elstow were ordered to appear before the Privy Council at Westminster. They were described as 'baylief, Williams, George Walton, Gent, Bunyan, Victualler, ...'; they were probably amongst men from many different counties called to give evidence concerning the ownership of land belonging to the dissolved religious houses.

John Bunyan's Father

Unfortunately after the 1550s there is then a gap in the story of the Elstow Bunyans. The parish registers of Elstow do not start until 1602 and even then some years are not complete.

The first entry for the Bunyan family is the birth of John Bunyan's

Commemorative stone marking site of cottage where John Bunyan was born at Harrowden. G9

father: 'Thomas the sonne of Thomas Bunyan'. It is probable that the baby's mother, John's grandmother, died in childbirth.

The Site at Elstow

The Bunyan cottage has long since disappeared; the probable site is marked by a commemorative stone reached by a pleasant walk along footpaths from either Harrowden or Elstow.

Village Life in the 17th Century

Village life was particularly hard for women. Apart from their continual pregnancies and the care of the house and family with no modern aids whatsoever in both town and country, they were often responsible for the care of the families' essential livestock.

If we are to try and understand what village life was like when John Bunyan was a boy, we must try and understand how very much things have changed since then, especially since as a country we have become independent of the weather.

In the late 20th century we are used to families whose daily routine revolves around the needs of the baby or toddler. During the 17th century, when most babies and young toddlers were fed at the breast in any convenient corner of the farmyard or field, it was the needs of the livestock which controlled the family timetable. Cows, and sometimes sheep, must be milked at a regular time, milk cooled as soon as possible, cheese made and turned at regular intervals, eggs collected from distant nests, broodies disciplined at one part of the year and carefully tended at another, ducks must be driven back from the stream and carefully housed, not just to keep them safe from foxes but to make sure that these careless birds laid their eggs in a spot where it was possible to collect them.

Survival economics amongst the poor involved collecting both wild and homegrown fruit and preserving it, growing and storing vegetables, collecting wool from the hedgerows, spinning and weaving, salting bacon, growing and collecting herbs, drying them, making medicines and ointments, gleaning a surprising amount of corn and when it was ground, preparing it for bread making.

Even though much of their arable land had been sold, like other village craftsmen the Bunyan family would have had a house cow, maybe a calf, an old pony or cart-horse, possibly a sheep or two, some geese and ducks on Cardington Brook, a few hens and maybe a hive of bees. Above all, as itinerant workers were obliged to leave the village for days at a time as they walked or rode around the surrounding villages and isolated farms, it was essential to have someone living in the cottage to look after the baby and the livestock.

It is not surprising that John's grandfather, father and John himself, quickly remarried when left alone with small children to care for.

As John's grandfather travelled the roads, selling his wares at farms and cottages, they may have realised how helpless people felt when their pots and pans sprang a leak or when an essential tool was broken. Wandering tinkers had a bad reputation. Being always on the road they had too many opportunities for thieving and selling stolen goods; farmers were more likely to discourage them than look forward to their arrival.

A brazier might be a local man, a respected craftsman who would take many of the repairs home to his own workshop and would be an asset to the area. People who had known Thomas as a young boy accompanying his father the chapman on his rounds, would have been delighted to have such a reliable craftsman calling on them.

Sign of 'The Three Fishes' at Turvey. A metal sign of this type would have been made by a brazier. C7

In 1624, when Thomas II was nearly twenty-one, he married Ann 'Purney' (Pinney), but she was buried on 13 April 1627 and six weeks later Thomas II married again.

The Marriage of John Bunyan's Parents

His new wife was Margaret Bentley, a village girl of his own age, whom he must have known all his life. She came from a very similar background but the Bunyan household may well have had an extra upstairs sleeping chamber fitted when Thomas II married for the first time. When Margaret's mother, Mrs Bentley, died five years later, she divided her clothes and furniture between her son and four daughters. Margaret, the eldest, was her executor and was to receive a special stool, her mother's little case of personal possessions and the residue of her estate.

The Birth of John Bunyan

Having settled in at 'Bunyan's End' with her new husband, her father-in-law, his wife and children, she was soon pregnant. On 30 November 1628 her son, John, was baptised, followed 15 months later by a daughter, whom they baptised Margaret. When John was nearly five years old, his brother William was born and the family was complete.

CHAPTER TWO

The Fight for Freedom of Worship

To understand the emotional struggles that John Bunyan underwent as a young man, we must take a look at the religious climate in which he grew up.

After the Reformation, the Church of England retained much of the pre-Reformation structure. There were still archbishops, bishops, archdeacons, priests and deacons. Parishes had their parish church and the rector or vicar was appointed by the patron of the living. There were, too, the same church courts, to ensure obedience to the church's laws by both clergy and laity.

However, what people were told to believe was now very different. The old belief, that salvation came from seeking God in the sacraments and by following his laws as mediated through the one Catholic Church, had gone. The doctrine of the Church of England was not strongly Calvinistic. Salvation came by faith, and faith came from reading the scriptures, and from hearing the scriptures expounded by reformed preachers.

Queen Elizabeth I and her ministers tried to make the national church into one which might be accepted by the moderates of both sides, so it retained some things from the medieval church, while being a reformed protestant body in doctrine. Even absence from Sunday service for which the standard fine was one shilling (approximately three days' wages) was quite often ignored if the offence was not too blatant.

The strongest party in the church were the Puritans, who believed the Bible to be all-important. They had no wish to be governed by bishops and archdeacons, who were not designated by the Bible. They felt that the parish minister should have the power to discipline all in his parish and not to be obliged to admit people who lived ungodly lives. They did not wish to perform ceremonies such as making the

Hinchinbroke House, Huntingdon, where James I met the puritan clergy of Bedfordshire, 1604.

Stained glass window in Bletsoe Church. Commemorating the 400th anniversary of the first printed Bible, in memory of Harry Cheetham, died 6 May 1938. E5

Wilden Rectory, now a private house but once the home of Francis Dillingham, one of the men responsible for the 'King James' translation of the Bible. H6

sign of the cross in baptism, wearing a surplice and using a ring in marriage, on the demand of the bishop.

When Queen Elizabeth died, King James of Scotland started on his progress south. A group of 16 'Puritan Ministers of the Lincoln Diocese', including Thomas Brightman of Haynes, met at Hinchin-brooke (near Huntingdon) and on 30 November 1604, presented James with a petition 'witnessed in their own handwriting' for the 'removal of abuses'.

King James received them politely and the following year set up a conference at Hampton Court, to listen to different shades of opinion concerning church government. He heard the views of the Puritans who wanted to reform the established church, and also the views of the more extreme groups, who believed that their leader should be selected by a local committee, and not ordained and wished on them by a distant bishop. King James was very shocked. He agreed to set up a panel to translate and publish the Bible in English but refused to even discuss the suggestions put forward by the extremists. Francis Dillingham, the rector of Wilden and Andrew Byng, vicar of Everton, were members of the above panel.

Two years before it was ordered that each parish priest must record not only the number of communicants in his parish but also the number of Roman Catholics (there were only 27 remaining in Bedfordshire, all in the north of the county) and the 'Non-conformists'. Only three priests in the whole county admitted to have the latter in their parishes, and of the 11 individuals recorded, six were at Elstow, 15 years before the birth of John Bunyan. Four were recorded at Southill and one at Harlington. These figures of 'non-conformity' depended entirely on the interpretation of the parish priest but the prosecution of both clergy and laity in the next few years, shows how inaccurate they were.

Excommunication

Not only were those excommunicated forbidden to attend church but they were isolated from their neighbours. In 1617 William Worrall, of Kempston, was charged because he continued to trade with Thomas Crawley of Luton after Crawley had been excommunicated for ordering his employees to do farm work on a Sunday. Contact with excommunicates was a punishable offence. John Glidall, fuller of

Cranfield, and Francis Crashop were fined because they employed one, namely Richard Barrett; Roger Perriam of Bedford was summoned because he dared to go courting one, Margaret Bennett; Robert Baker, the Stevington parish clerk, got into trouble for burying one and Anne Skevington of Turvey was herself excommunicated for attending the funeral of her previously excommunicated husband!

The scattered cases of devout believers, looking for freedom of worship and risking imprisonment rather than attend the parish church, come from all over the county; they include John Crawley of Kensworth and William Shackspeare of Odell.

Although King James encouraged the playing of games after Divine Service, in many Bedfordshire parishes the local church authorities demanded that the whole day must still be kept free of secular employment or entertainment. Men from Barford and several other places were punished for watching football on a Sunday and from Renhold for playing nine-holes. Roger White of Risely and Roger Kinge of Shelton were punished for working with their horses, the Woburn barber, Peter Lord, was reported for cutting hair and several men were caught working in Bedford. These offences are recorded from all over the county and in many cases one can see contempt for the parish church and vicar rather than for the Lord's Day.

Poorly Paid Clergy

In some villages, the clergy no longer felt it necessary to revere the buildings in which they worshipped God. It is recorded that the curate at Woburn allowed bear baiting to take place in the church, that the rector at Carlton would tie up his horse in the chancel during service and that for three years running, the rector of Knotting, his son and the churchwardens, encouraged the congregation to go into the church on Shrove Tuesday and gamble at cockfights!

Another cause of concern was the low standard of clergy appointed to some of the very poorly paid livings in the diocese. Although in some parishes there were priests who could produce sermons and other writing fit for publication there were many others where the incumbent would only preach on special occasions and some where there were no sermons at all. The Puritan forms of discipline and worship were on the whole popular in Bedfordshire, where many people wanted a 'Bible based' service and a good preacher.

*Knotting Church where at one
time the rector allowed cockfighting to take place on Shrove
Tuesday.* E3

*Chancel Gates at Knotting
Church, put up when
cockfighting was forbidden.* E3

King Charles I was the first King of England to be brought up in the Anglican faith. He was in no way a Puritan, but whole-heartedly of the other, more Catholic party in the Church of England, the Arminians. These felt that the believer received God's grace through the sacraments of the church, mediated by the priest. The Communion Service to them was more than a mere commemoration. They could not share the Puritans' trust in the power of sermons to change a man's heart. Thus to exalt the sacrament, they wanted the holy table or altar to be returned to the chancel, as before the Reformation. In many churches it now stood in the nave and they wanted it to be railed off. There was another political difference between the two groups. Puritanism as proposed by the gentry would lead to a Presbyterian church, largely free from the King's control. The old structure with episcopacy and church courts, kept supreme power in the crown.

One of the main promoters of these ideas and a close friend and adviser of King Charles, was William Laud, Bishop of London. In 1633 Charles made him Archbishop of Canterbury and as the over-large diocese of Lincoln was known to be lapsing in many of the points which he held as essential, he immediately planned a 'metropolitan visitation'. He sent two officials around each county in the diocese of Lincoln, not only to enquire into the maintainance of church buildings and property but also into 'the conduct of clergy and laity' and into the controversial subject of 'non-conformity'. This included a check that any adult who failed to attend their own parish church on a Sunday, regardless of whether or not a sermon would be preached, would be automatically punished. With their emphasis on the Sacrament of Holy Communion, they were also checking that in every church the altar was permanently fixed at the east end of the church and separated from the congregation by rails. With their requirement of ceremonial within the service, they were checking that the priest in church always wore required dress (i.e. the surplice) and used the traditional symbols such as making the sign of the cross where the Book of Common Prayer required it.

The Preachers

Dr John Farmery, Chancellor of the Diocese, warned the officers before they set out that the people of Bedfordshire and Buckingham-shire were the sort 'that run from their own parishes after affected

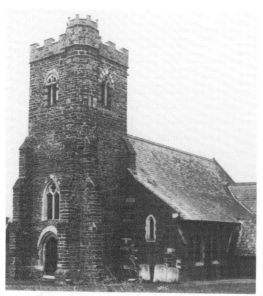

Top left, *Haynes Church where Mr Shirley, the puritan vicar, refused to wear his surplice when taking services.* H11. Top right, *Whipsnade Church and Tower built over 30 years before the birth of John Bunyan.* E19 Below left, *Whipsnade Rectory, once the home of the puritan minister Nathaniel Holmes.* E19 Below right, *Church at Odell. The puritan rector, Peter Bulkley, was obliged to leave in 1635 and sail to America.* C4

preachers ...'. He also recorded the revealing fact that the 'new Recorder of Bedford' (that would be the Earl of Bolingbroke or somebody representing him) had excused these people, had described the lecturers as 'godly men' and had commented that if men were 'troubled for going to hear a sermon when their minister at home did not preach, it would breed a scab in the kingdom'.

Later evidence suggests that many of the landed gentry were to some degree sympathetic to this desire to hear sermons. At Hemel Hempstead (see below) the lord of the manor provided for 'a lecturer' in his will.

Mr Shirley, the vicar of Haynes was reported for 'not conforming' to the services laid down by the established church. Several local clergy got into trouble because the commissioners confessed that, although they suspected several other priests of 'inconformitre' e.g. Nathaniel Holmes of Whipsnade, Zachary Symmes of Dunstable and possibly Samuel Fisher of Leighton Buzzard, they could get no proof! (see below). However, Peter Bulkeley of Odell was not so lucky; he was absent from his parish when the commission reached Bedford and was summoned to meet them at Aylesbury. Having inherited a parish already accustomed to his Puritan father, Bulkeley was convinced that the belief of those taking part in the service was of more importance than what he wore or the method in which he conducted the services, he refused to make excuses.

He confessed that '... he never used the surplisse, or the crosse in Baptisme' and he was ordered to appear at the High Commissioner's Court in November. Both his patrons, the St John family and the Bishop of Lincoln, had showed tolerance to this devoted parish priest but now he must conform or go. The following year he and his family sailed for America (see below). Change followed change. The tolerant Bishop Williams was removed and Laud's own officers began to administer the diocese.

Some time around August 1637 Walter Walker became commissary (assistant) to John Hacket, Archdeacon of Bedford. Hacket was promoted and Walker was then reporting directly to Lincoln and so to Archbishop Laud. One of his first actions was to put an end to the cockfighting at Knotting and other such abuses. He then turned his attention to those churches which were openly ignoring Laud's commands concerning the position of altars and altar rails. He started with St Paul's Bedford and demanded that they place their communion table standing north and south, on a raised dais at the end of the chancel; also that it should be railed off from the congregation who should come to the rails to take communion, kneeling. They were obliged to carry out his orders but he was furious to discover that the vicar, John Bradshaw, left the rails and came down amongst the congregation to adminster communion. Bradshaw was ordered to appear before the High Commission and Walker himself tried to lead communicants to kneel at the rails but several still refused. One of the churchwardens who supported Bradshaw when he appeared before the High Commission was John Eston (see below), who was to become a friend and supporter of John Bunyan.

That there was plenty for Walker to do in Bedfordshire is shown by the 'faults' uncovered by the next visitation ordered by Archbishop Laud in April 1638. John Gwin who was the vicar of Cople, put there by the Dean and Chapter of Christ Church Oxford, was an ardent supporter of Archbishop Laud and several of his parishioners were summoned because they regularly attended church in the neighbouring village of Cardington. Frank Coles was reported because, at a friend's funeral, he made fun of Gwin's attire, remarking that his surplice made him look like a morris dancer! The lord of the manor, Sir Samuel Luke, who was patron of the living of St Paul's, above, did not approve of Gwin or enjoy his services. Wood End Farm (on the site of Luke's house) is about one-and-a-half miles from the village church, most of it down a long lane now covered with tarmac but in 1638 probably deep rutted with wet mud in winter and powdery dust in summer. The way through to Cardington today is a green lane, and in those days it can have been no better than the road to Cople. Nevertheless in July of that year, Sir Samuel Luke appealed to Laud that he might be allowed to attend the more distant church because of the 'foulness of the way' to Gwin's church at Cople.

Walter Walker undoubtedly had a difficult time in Bedfordshire but maybe he was the sort of man who enjoyed a challenge. Examples of his accusations include those who still refused to wear a surplice as at Stondon, those who refused to bow at the name of Jesus at Kempston and those who put too much emphasis on the ministry of preaching as at Bromham.

Elstow Church

John Bunyan was six years old when Archbishop Laud's officials first visited Bedfordshire and ten years old when Sir Samuel Luke and several other parishioners were resisting the 'Laudian' vicar at nearby Cople. The vicar of Elstow who reported the six non-conformists in 1603, had died but his successor, the Rev. John Kelly, may also have been 'hostile to Puritans' as he escaped criticism. We know of only three parish clerks at the Abbey Church of St Mary and St Helena between 1589 and 1750. John Sharpe (d.1642) was very active and upset several parishioners including Thomas Bunyan I, John's grandfather; he appears to have reported any misdemeanours which came to his ears.

However, these complaints which were scattered across the north and middle of the county were as nothing to the combined resistance in the south and in the neighbouring Hertfordshire villages. Although the Bishop's visitation only uncovered one man, John Pryor, who persistently stayed away from All Saints Caddington, in fact, Dunstable and its neighbouring villages were in a state of rebellion.

The Dunstable Non-conformists

For some reason, the vicar of the Priory Church of St Peter, Dunstable, did not complete the questionnaire of 1603 and during the early years of the century, parishioners from Dunstable do not appear in the records of the Archdeacon's Court. The reason for this was probably because the vicar, John Richardson BA, was himself a Puritan. He was repeatedly summoned to the bishop's court because he performed his services without the ceremony demanded by the established church.

In the surrounding villages, the clergy were unsympathetic to the 'non conformists' and in 1609 a strict conformist priest was appointed in Dunstable.

The efforts of thirty or more families from Dunstable and Upper Houghton, to drive out the Rev. Edward Alport is too long a story to include here. However, the scandal caused in 1618, when he prosecuted 26 men and four ladies for such mixed offences as holding a drunken brawl under his bedroom window, refusing to allow his locum into the church and then reporting him for leaving the parish on a Sunday so that no service could be held, and holding him up to ridicule by baptising a sheep in his name and putting it into the pulpit to preach a sermon(!) must have still been common talk in the fields and ale-houses when John Bunyan was young.

Meanwhile, at St Antholin's Church in London, a committee of wealthy merchants were supporting, encouraging and generally helping to train a team of clergymen who wished, within the established church, to lead a congregation in the faithful worship of God, without the strict discipline of the prayer book service. In 1625, this committee managed to buy for £350 the 'Impropriation pertaining to the Priory Church of St Peter, Dunstable'. In other words they had the right to appoint a clergyman to the living. Their choice was Zachary Symmes, a young man who had recently trained at Emmanuel College, Cambridge. He fitted in very well with the people of Dunstable and for seven years, until the committee who supported him were dismantled by Archbishop Laud, the Priory Church of St Peter, Dunstable, was a non-conformist place of worship.

It appears that he stayed on in Dunstable, supported by the congregation, for another two years, until the activities of the Archbishop's officials made it impossible for him to remain. He then sailed to America with at least five other Dunstable families and settled in Charleston, Massachusetts. He was connected with the Old South Church, Boston where his daughter, Huldah who was born in Dunstable in August 1632, was married.

He died on 4 February 1670 and engraved on his memorial stone is the couplet:

> A prophet lies under this stone,
> His words shall live tho' he be gone.

He was replaced in Dunstable by William Peddar who at the outbreak of war went off to join the Royalist army.

Maybe the stricter non-conformists among the congregation had found some other preacher.

Dissatisfaction at Kensworth

Bunyan was about six years old when Zachary Symmes left Dunstable, William Peddar arrived and Dr John Farmery warned Laud's officials that the people of Bedfordshire ran off from their own parish churches to listen to other preachers.

The following year, Laud sent a special report to King Charles that his officials had also found 'troupes' of people refusing to attend church at Kensworth in Hertfordshire. Who was the preacher in 1634 who attracted crowds of listeners out on Kensworth Cross Roads or to Dunstable Downs?

The vicar was John Syddall, who had been living in the vicarage for nearly 20 years. He had married some years previously and already had seven small children. (He would have four more before he died ten years later.) Being a strong supporter of Archbishop Laud, he also suffered great distress from a rebellious congregation.

Church of St Mary the Virgin, Kensworth. F18

CHAPTER THREE

John Bunyan's Boyhood in Elstow

In the reign of Charles I, when church attendance was compulsory, Bunyan's family do not appear on the list of those fined at the Archdeacon's court, so we can assume that the young John Bunyan accompanied his parents to Elstow parish church each Sunday morning. There, willingly or not, he would have taken part in the church services of that time.

Unfortunately, we know very little about Bunyan's boyhood; if only we knew more we might find it easier to understand him as a man. Also, we must not put too much reliability on the little pieces of information that he lets drop in his spiritual autobiography, *Grace Abounding*.

We can visit the beautiful church of St Helena and sit quietly in the half-light and try to think back through the years. Listen to the bells in their free-standing bell tower and imagine a cheerful young man tolling away with pleasure and musical excitement, or try to see inside the tortured mind of a slightly older man, hurrying past the church, and, as his problems twist his brain, breaking into a run as he imagines the bells breaking free and the stones of the tower tumbling down onto his head and shoulders. The stained glass windows are new but the brightly-coloured funeral hatchments were already there and before the Civil War there would have been colourful pictures on the walls and perhaps large, painted boards representing Moses and Aaron standing on either side of a list of the Ten Commandments. A royal coat of arms, similar to that hanging over the door today, would have been painted just after the Civil War.

Although the wonderfully preserved High Street is spoiled by the noise of traffic, and the Moot Hall is uncomfortably close to that noise,

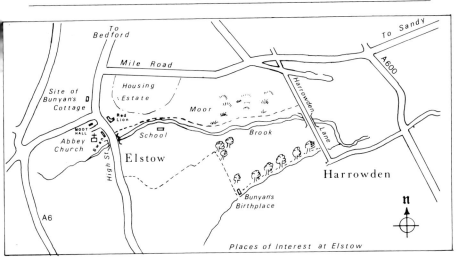

Places of Interest at Elstow

Black and white, timber-framed cottages of Elstow High Street. F9

the area around the church, what remains of the Hillersden Mansion and the field under which the nunnery lies is quiet and peaceful. From there, we can look across the fields to the black timbers and white plaster of the old cottages, some of which would have housed the friends with whom John Bunyan went to school.

School Days

Neither John's grandfather or father signed their wills with anything other than a cross but we must remember that these may have been made at a time of illness, and to be able to write was much rarer than being able to read.

As itinerant workers, they must have been more aware than most village people of all the changes that were going on and the general unrest locally and nationally. They must also have realised that reading and writing would be of use to a craftsman and so, as Bunyan tells us, '... it pleased God to put it into their hearts to put me to school, to learn both to read and write, the which I also attained, according to the rate of other poor men's children'.

From this we can assume that he was familiar with long passages from the Bible, Old Testament stories and other religious books.

Although in 1563 Sir William Harpur had given land to preserve what has become known as 'The Harpur School' at Bedford and, sometime before 1631, Sir Francis Clerke had endowed a Free School at Houghton Conquest, it is unlikely that Bunyan attended these.

In most villages education or the lack of it depended on the vicar; some suitable person would teach reading and a little writing in a space provided at the church, usually for a few pence a week paid for by the parents. Whether this was on weekday evenings or even during the day depended on local circumstances. Occasionally, some man or woman approved of by the vicar might run a small school in their own home.

Nearly, if not all, of this education was based on the Bible, books of homilies and other such adult books. No wonder that Bunyan goes on to tell us that he soon lost the little learning that he had gained and that when he himself wrote *A Book For Boys and Girls** the short spiritual messages were wrapped up in verses about animals and such earthly things as 'A Penny Loaf'.

**Divine Emblems, or Temporal Things Spiritualized.*

Education at Home and on the Road

John Bunyan must from an early age have helped with the work around the cottage, fed the animals, collected firewood, chopped it and helped with the dozens of routine and seasonal jobs. From keeping his father's workshop tidy and working the bellows he would have progressed to doing simple repair jobs. How he must have longed for the chance to go out and return the finished work, or better still to go out for days at a time, carrying a pack for his grandfather. Surely he got more education from the people he met on the road than from his little time at school? There were on the roads a whole sub-culture of itinerant workers of which his father represented the craftsmen and his grandfather the salesmen. He must have known other petty chapmen like his grandfather, lace dealers and others, who would have been well known to their customers, as would the higglers with their kidney-shaped 'back baskets' calling to collect the spare eggs or cheese and who might be persuaded to take a couple of rabbits into market. He would also have met traders who travelled great distances with their

The Knife Grinder. An itinerant craftsman working in Bedfordshire c.1973.

horses and carts buying up spare corn or 'Scotsmen' and similar who crossed the country selling cheap linen cloth from the mills. These would probably be strangers and, with their 'foreign' accents and strange ways, were normally treated with suspicion, as were the gypsies and seasonal agriculture workers, but their very unfamiliarity must have been fascinating to the young John Bunyan. Many times he must have been sent out onto the 'Kings Highway' near Cardington to wait for the carrier and get him to buy or sell something as he went down through Luton. Or his father may have told him to wait for the cart and pay the carrier to drop off a finished repair job at the nearest inn to a customer's house.

When he was walking to and fro to school, he would have had the chance to talk to the many travellers who stopped at the various inns in Elstow High Street and no doubt looked forward to the days when stalls were set up on the green and the village was alive with the noise and bustle of stall holders shouting their wares and with customers laughing and joking or occasionally shouting abuse. Not only farmers' wives and cottagers but servants from the big houses gathered around the stalls because Elstow had a well known and prosperous fair.

A Country Childhood

A country boy from a happy home with a sister only 15 months younger than himself, a brother young enough to be his willing slave and a father who was frequently away from home, the young John Bunyan had both a lot of freedom and a lot of responsibility. No doubt he could earn a few small coins by gathering nuts and blackberries or digging the garden for some rheumaticky cottager.

Judging by his children's book of *Divine Emblems*, he had had experience of fishing and bird trapping, both of which were a source of income. It may have been on a fishing trip to the River Ouse that he had his great adventure referred to in *Grace Abounding*, when he fell into the river and nearly drowned.

Soon after 1700, Celia Fiennes visited Bedford and noted that the river contained so many pike, perch and tench that people stored them in a form of basket along the riverside. She also writes about the many little boats chained to the sides of the river 'for their diversion'. Maybe the boys 'borrowed' one of these or made a coracle, tried fishing further down in deeper water, and tipped it over!

His Love of Nature Shows in his Writing

Many years later, when he was sitting writing in prison he repeatedly referred to the rising of the sun. Only a country boy, who had risen to milk the cow, or to run across the wet fields before it got light, could use examples such as these to express the wonders of divine light.

Meditations Upon Peep of Day

I Oft, though it be peep of day, don't know
Whether 'tis night, whether 'tis day or no.
I fancy that I see a little light,
But cannot yet distinguish day from night;

I hope, I doubt, but steady yet I be not,
I am not at a point, the sun I see not.
Thus 'tis with such who grace but now possest,
They know not yet if they be cursed or blest.

*Upon the Sun's Reflection Upon
the Clouds in a Fair Morning*

Look yonder, ah! me thinks mine eyes do see
Clouds edged with silver, as fine garments be;
They look as if they saw that golden face
That makes black clouds most beautiful with grace.
Unto the saints' sweet incense, or their prayer,
These smoky curdled clouds I do compare.
For as these clouds seem edged, or laced with gold,
Their prayers return with blessings manifold.

We can learn as much, if not more, about the young John Bunyan from these poems as we can from *Grace Abounding*.

How many salesmen, craftsmen, preachers and others have set out on the road before it got light and have peered at the sky, thinking about the day ahead?

Upon a Lowering Morning

Well, with the day I see the clouds appear,
And mix the light with darkness everywhere;
This threatening is, to travellers that go
Long journeys, slabby rain they'll have, or snow.

Else, while I gaze, the sun doth with his beams
Belace the clouds, as 'twere with bloody streams;
This done, they suddenly do watery grow,
And weep, and pour their tears out where they go.

Poems about birds and fishes, moles, snails, flies, butterflies and frogs.

The frog by nature is both damp and cold,
Her mouth is large, her belly much will hold.

He thinks of all the different types of men and meditates about eggs; eggs which are rotten, eggs which can produce domestic chicks, or wild fowl, or snakes or even spiders.

He thinks of men who go around boasting of their good deeds and compares them with cackling hens who, as soon as they lay an egg, spread the news of what they have done.

About the yard she cackling now doth go,
To tell what 'twas she at her nest did do.

The Troubled Boy

In his introduction to *Grace Abounding* Bunyan writes about the time that he was without God, when it was his 'delight to be taken captive by the devil at his will'. How this affected both his 'heart and his life' so that he had few equals in '. . . cursing, swearing, lying and blaspheming the holy name of God'.

This type of thoughtless, careless and irreverent behaviour became so much a natural part of his life that at night he would awake, scared and frightened by fearful dreams. His actual statements are extremely brief but they are very precise and we can at least try to put together a picture of the tormented boy.

It appears that during the hours of daylight he managed to forget his problems and thoroughly enjoy his bad behaviour. It was only when he was asleep that he would dream of wicked spirits who had come to take him away. When he woke up with these terrors fresh in his mind, he would lie there in his familiar bed, heart pounding and drift from dreams of devils into thoughts of his future. Life in his day was so short and so precarious, even for a ten-year-old-boy. Death could be waiting just around the corner – if he died would he descend straight to the torments of hell-fire? Would it be his lot, 'to be found at last among those who are there bound down with chains and bonds of darkness unto the judgement of the great day'?

These are the words of a man in his thirties; the actual nightmares and night panics of a young boy are almost beyond words, and they didn't only attack him at night.

As we have seen, the Puritan beliefs that dancing was wrong and that the playing of the most innocent games on a Sunday was wicked, were strongly held in Bedfordshire. In 1639 when Bunyan was 11, Christopher Hall was appointed as vicar of St Helena. Many years later he may have been Bunyan's model for 'Mr Facing-both-ways' because during his incumbancy he managed to satisfy both Puritan and High Church parties! He is known to have supported the local feeling against games on Sundays.

Bunyan's Passages of Autobiography

Henri Talon, in his book *John Bunyan*, devotes a chapter to discussing not only the small shreds of possible autobiography scattered within the text of *Grace Abounding* but also to summing up and comparing the opinions of many other writers as to how far we should trust these fragments; also, how far we can use this book and others of Bunyan's writings when we are looking for the cause of the emotional distress of his childhood and the religious struggles and conversion of his later years. He wisely reminds us that,

> . . . each of us notices only the things we are prepared to see; that, to a certain extent, the glance creates the thing seen, and that introspection, like the vision of the external world, involves an unconscious choice.

I am no theologian, no psychologist or literary scholar, but I have both experience of, and love of, village people, village churches and village life and I have learnt that 'people are people' regardless of their background or the century in which they live, so may I suggest a few *theories* from the story that I can read between the lines of Bunyan's writing.

Thatched cottage still standing on the corner of the Old Harrowden Road and A.600. G/H9

Reading between the Lines

Young people like to conform with their peers and they want their parents to conform with the parents of their friends. As early as 1603, when there were only 11 non-conformists recorded in the whole of Bedfordshire, six of them lived in Elstow. By the time that John was 11, many of the people of Elstow, including the vicar, the Rev. Christopher Hall, were either 'Puritan' in their beliefs (or prepared to accept Puritan principles) or claimed to believe that every word of the Old and New Testaments, including the Ten Commandments, should be obeyed.

There are few things more damaging to a young mind than conflict. Every Sunday, at least once and sometimes twice (and maybe at school), he was confronted with the brightly painted Ten Commandments.

Commandment 3: 'Thou shalt not take the Name of the Lord thy God in vain: for the Lord will not hold him guiltless that taketh his Name in vain'.

Commandment 4: 'Remember that thou keep holy the Sabbath Day. Six days shalt thou labour, and do all that thou hast to do, but the seventh day is the Sabbath of the Lord thy God. In it thou shalt do no manner of work, thou, and thy son, and thy daughter, ... the Lord blessed the seventh day, and hallowed it'.

Commandment 5: 'Honour thy father and thy mother, that thy days may be long in the land which the Lord thy God giveth thee'.

But what if your father doesn't keep the Sabbath holy, and does take the name of God in vain? Where then does your loyalty lie? And supposing all your friends play games on the Sabbath and swear in a way which would have been quite acceptable a century before but is now taboo – what do you do then?

Supposing you go to school and read dreadful stories about God punishing His people because He loves them; you go to church and hear the minister preaching long sermons about the wicked who are heading for hell and damnation. You read the fourth Commandment forbidding all work on the Sabbath and ordering you to keep it holy and you read the fifth Commandment which orders you to honour your father and mother but your father doesn't keep the Sabbath holy! He cuts wood, mends the roof, puts up fences and does all the jobs that get neglected when he is out on the road and, although he daren't go off walking on the highway in case he is prosecuted (see below), in the privacy of Harrowden he may well finish off an important job ready for an early start on Monday morning.

For a sensitive and highly intelligent boy, there must have been so many conflicts.

Suppose, to please his father, he gets up early, goes out across the fields to an open space on high ground, puts down a handful of corn and chaff, sets up some mirrors to distract the attention of the birds that come down to feed and then he catches them with a net, ignoring their terrified struggles. He then takes them home where his earthly father praises and maybe rewards him but when later in the day he reluctantly goes off to school he learns that Jesus loves all animals and is saddened by every sparrow that falls – and he can't help thinking about all those poor sparrows struggling in the net.

He thinks about the other village boys and how cruelly they treat sparrows and, if he is honest, doesn't he get excited by the feeling of power over the struggling birds?

They weren't all sparrows of course, the fowler in Bedford market would give you much more for finches and the inns much more for larks than the churchwardens would give for sparrows. Should he have kept the birds which would help to pay for a new pair of boots to wear for school and church and let the sparrows go? But whatever would Mr Sharpe, the churchwarden, say if he heard that John had let the sparrows go? They thieved so much corn at harvest time and Mr Sharpe should know what to do to please God, because he had been churchwarden ever since John's father had been a little boy. Most of the village people were more frightened of him than they were of the vicar!

Whatever would the other boys have said if he had tried to let the sparrows free? It was the same with playing games on Sunday. During the night he would lay trembling on his truckle bed under the thatch, trying not to wake young William and let him see how upset he was. As the dreams gradually faded, he would promise God that he would never play tip cat, his favourite Sunday game, again.

Still too frightened to get out of bed, he would lay there, hands clasped together and pray. When it was nearly light and his tormenting dreams had faded, he would jump out of bed, put on his coat and shoes, collect a bucket from the kitchen and head off down the lane to the place where the house cow was tethered. By the time that he had finished milking and was hurrying back home to get the fire alight and the kettle on, his mind had switched to how, if he tried to avoid temptation and didn't spend the afternoon on the Green, he could avoid spending his precious free time in cleaning out the barn ready for the new season's hay. It was no good reminding his father that the Sabbath was holy and that it said on the wall at church '... thou shalt do no manner of work, thou, and thy son ...'. All his father would say, was, 'The better the day, the better the deed'!

Just as he was nearing the house, he met his friend, who was guiding his geese down to their grazing patch by the stream, 'See you round behind the hall after service, John.'

'Right Tom – see you there.'

And that was that; it was no good pretending that he was strong enough to meet the others and not join in the games, even if they would let him!

It was all right if your parents actually believed all the things that

The River Ouse at Bedford following the heavy rain of January 1988. F8

Mr Hall said in church, then no one expected you to play games, or clean out the barn either. Honour your heavenly father or honour your earthly father? Play tip cat or clean out the barn?

If he asked his mother what to do, she would tell him to help his father and keep away from those 'troublemakers on the Green' or she might ask him to take his brother William up to the village to see his grandparents. That would be fine if only it wasn't Sunday; they could get the chap books out of his grandfather's bag and he would read William a story but not on Sunday. Oh no, his grandmother would never let them read adventure stories on a Sunday; she'd get the Bible out and in no time at all she'd have William sitting on a stool beside her while John stumbled his way through the Psalms. No stories about battles and foreign kings, on Sundays something more 'holy', that is to say more boring. Long boring passages that appeared to have no beginning and no end. He liked the one about being fed in a green pasture because it made him think about picnics in the watermeadows beside the River Ouse, when he went fishing at Bedford. He also liked the one that told him to lift up his eyes unto the hills if he needed help; he often thought about it when he was out on the road and caught sight of the line of hills right down in the south of the county.

Apart from a few like that, there were far too many with passages that he found frightening or worrying.

> For my soul is full of trouble: and my
> life draweth nigh into hell.
> I am counted as one of them that go down
> into the pit: and I have been even as
> man that hath no strength.

His grandmother would sit there spinning, because after all, spinning wouldn't count as work if she was listening to the Bible. John was never sure if she actually listened to the words or whether she only wanted him to read to her so that her conscience would let her spin! They were reading through the Book of Psalms and each time they finished John had to mark the place with a piece of grubby lace that his sister Margaret had made for grandmother's birthday. When they read passages such as:

> He turned their waters into blood: and
> slew their fish
> Their land brought forth frogs: yea, even
> in their King's chambers.

he tried to miss them out because otherwise brother William would shriek with laughter and ask silly questions about there being frogs in the King's chambers and then grandmother would get cross and send them out to the shed to see their grandfather who would want them to cut the hedge or dig the garden and then the whole street would know that they were working on a Sunday. No, it was easier to keep out of everybody's way and go and play tip cat on the Green and, if the dreams returned, he must put up with it. It was easy to be brave in daylight!

Why then, in this happy family home, with enough to eat, enough learning to read the books that he enjoyed and more than average freedom did he suffer from such terrible nightmares?

CHAPTER FOUR

Life in a Bedfordshire Village

Before we leave the young John Bunyan we should get some idea of what the farms and villages were like that he visited with his father and grandfather.

The picture on page 14 is said to be a drawing of John Bunyan's birthplace. It shows a familiar agricultural cottage with at least two rooms and a scullery on the ground floor. Even if the nearest room has been added on since his boyhood, by 17th century standards, it must have been a most comfortable cottage and as John travelled around he would have seen far humbler dwellings.

The so called 'hall' was still the main room in most cottages although many of them would have had a separate bed-sitting room divided off at one end, with a store room or second bedroom over it. From the numerous surviving 17th-century inventories we can get a very good idea of the way these cottages were furnished.

Changes had been taking place for some time. Most houses had a chimney although Bunyan may well have visited the occasional cottage where the smoke from the open fire found its way out through a shutter in the roof. Even where there was a separate 'kitchen' or 'backhouse' outside the back door, the main cooking was still done over the hall fire. Although during Bunyan's boyhood most cottages had their bed-sitting room or 'bedchamber', it was still quite normal to have one or more beds in the hall. Furniture was also changing; there were still far more stools and benches than there were chairs and more dual purpose chest/seats than there were cupboards but the quality of furniture was improving. Joiners were producing 'jointed' tables, supported by a special frame, much superior to the rough boards which had previously been set up on trestles. The old furniture wasn't thrown away but stored or used in the servants' room. As cottagers had more possessions so there was a greater need for space and storage.

Small cottage at Silsoe with extension. G/H13

17th-century bed displayed at The Moot Hall, Elstow. F9 Right, *'Jointed' benches, stool and table displayed at The Moot Hall, Elstow.* F9

Sometimes separate work rooms such as 'milk rooms' and 'butteries' were built but more often they were separated from the hall by partitions. In either case simple plank ceilings were made and the 'attic', often reached by a ladder, was used for storage. Where there was a shortage of floor space some cottagers made simple 'attics' in the roof space of the main hall.

The Labourers' Homes

The houses and furniture of people described as 'labourers' varied as much as the number of their livestock. Nicholas Groome of Wingfield had a table, forms, a chair and two stools in his hall and a cupboard in which to keep his pieces of pewter and brass. His pot-hangers, pots and very few cooking utensils were kept in the hall but he also had a 'butterie' where he kept the necessary barrels and bowls used for brewing his beer and a 'kitchin' for preparing and salting bacon. His bedsteads were in a separate chamber together with his clothes and very simple household linen, stored in two chests. Outside he had three 'bease', a bullock, three pigs, two beehives, ten hens and a cockerel. Apart from the bees, these all lived in a barn where he also kept their grain and hay.

Most village householders kept some livestock and men described as 'labourers' did not necessarily live less comfortably than craftsmen. Although Thomas Robinson of Cotton End, near Elstow, kept his labouring tools such as mattock, grindstone, scythe and pitchforks in the hall, together with the woollen wheel and most of their limited collection of cooking utensils, these may have been carefully stored at one end. At the living end he had painted cloths on the wall, a chair for father, a child's chair and a cradle. The family had both wooden and 'latten' (brass alloy) candlesticks and one can imagine a winter evening in years gone by when mother sat spinning beside the fire, occasionally taking her foot from the pedal to rock the cradle, a toddler playing with pieces of wood, safely strapped in its chair, while the older children sorted and carded wool or helped father make pegs or mend nets for catching rabbits.

The family owned an 'earthen warming pan' so towards bedtime an older girl, having heated it with embers from the fire, would have taken a candle and gone to warm the beds in the cold sleeping room behind the partition. In 1620, when Thomas Robinson was an old man living alone, this room was known as the 'wash house'. It contained his bed and two other old beds and three chests containing all the spare bed clothes. These were in a corner of the room, again lined with painted cloths. At the other end were the salting trough, two 'Fletches' of bacon and a pile of tanned calf skins. At the same time he had rigged up a loft of planks over the room which now held the unused cheese press 'and other lumber'. Outside he had a barn, hay, two beasts, two geese, three hens, a cock and some growing pullets.

Many craftsmen lived in similar, humble cottages. Simon of Tempsford, weaver, had a hall; three beds and four chests in his chamber and a third room known as the milkhouse where he kept his 'weavers lowme with workinge geares' at one end and cooking, cheese-making and bacon-salting implements at the other. No attics but again two house cows and a calf, a bullock, three pigs and four sheep. He also had two acres of peas and half an acre of barley.

Farmhouses

Two farms which Bunyan would have visited with his grandfather and father were those of George Edwards at Cotton End and William Burden of Silsoe. When their fathers died c. 1618, both described themselves as 'yeomen' but their farms and farm houses were very different.* Whereas Edwards' hall was a comfortable kitchen cum-sitting room, Burden's was more of a dining room; there were painted cloths on his wall, shelves where he displayed his 28 pieces of pewter, his candlesticks and salt cellars. A chamber pot was kept in a handy cupboard. In addition he had a comfortable, decorated parlour which appears to have been used as a dining room with a 'drawing table' which could be decreased in size to make room for a very comfortable feather bed with a 'matt cord' cover for daytime use. The second room at Cotton End was named a 'lodging chamber'. It was also decorated; it contained two comfortable beds and a good supply of spare sheets and other household linen. Most of the cooking must have taken place in the hall although he had several other small rooms. The one named 'kitchen' contained an empty chicken coop and all the necessities for

*The pictures opposite are of a private house at Silsoe which may well be part of the 17th century farm and of Wilhamstead Manor Farm which may have been the home of the Edwards family.

Wilshamstead Manor Farm. Pebble-dash covers the original timber frame. Contemporary barn. G10

Taberte Farm Silsoe, Back view, 1987. G/H13

cheese making. In the 'bolting house' was a salting trough, wheat meal trough, butter churn, and various sacks, bottles and pails. The usual tools were stored in the loft over this room. Then came the 'milkehouse' which was partly furnished as a dairy and cheese making room and partly as a cooking room. There were numerous pots, pans and kettles made from various materials and not only four salt cellars but also a spice morter and a 'chafinge dishe' which when filled with hot embers could be used to keep the farmer's meals hot if he was late in to meals.

The kitchen at Silsoe must have been like those we see in museums. A long table with two chairs, stools of various sizes, brass saucepans, kettles, bowls, chafing dish, skimmer, ladles and candlesticks, all arranged on shelves with a pestle and mortar. There were four spits, a pair of andirons to support the logs as they burnt and pot-hangers and hooks to support the pots and pans. A frying pan, dripping pan, fire shovel and a pair of bellows were kept near the fire place. There may well have been a dresser* as there were two dozen trenchers (wooden plates), one dozen dishes, six pewter spoons and 'two jugges to drinke in'.

In addition to this there were a range of adjoining buildings; 'the backhouse' was equipped to brew beer for the household, make cheese and sift the wheat meal to make bread flour. Four flitches of bacon hung from the ceiling. The 'drinke house' held eight barrels, two firkins, a wooden barrel stand and three leather bottles, together with cards for wool and the shepherds' equipment such as a pitch kettle and branding iron, there was also a pile of rough hemp and 'hetchells' for combing it. This Silsoe farm house, called 'Taberte', was, in 1619, rented from the Earl of Kent, at Wrest Park, for £40 per year. By the standards of the day it was exceptionally comfortable.

Small Manor Houses

While he was still a boy and accompanying his father on his journeys, John Bunyan would have visited farm houses and the kitchen quarters of many of the large houses of the county. With his grandfather, the chapman, he may well have been allowed into the hall or even the

---

*If this was attached to the wall it would have been ignored when the inventory was made.

parlour, while the children or the lady of the house examined the pins, ribbon, lace and small toys which were for sale.

Despite its undoubted warmth and comfort, it is probable that the whole Bunyan cottage would have fitted inside the great hall of the new Hillersden mansion house. It is, therefore, no wonder that, looking back over the years and thinking of the crowded cottage at Harrowden or his elderly, rheumaticky grandfather with his probably none too clean cottage by the Green and remembering the struggle that his father had to make a living during the dangerous and difficult days of the Civil War, he probably felt justified in writing, 'my father's house being of that rank that is meanest and most despised of all the families in the land'.

Although we know that there is still a great difference between the homes of the very poor and the very rich in England today, houses without a bathroom are more rare than mid-17th century houses without a chimney. Today we are more likely to compare the number of bedrooms, the number of bathrooms, the number and quality of television sets and other household possessions rather than their presence or absence. So we cannot begin to imagine the culture difference in 17th century Bedfordshire.

We have seen that an exceptional farmhouse such as 'Taberte' at Silsoe, may have had four or five rooms with a fireplace but of the 88 houses listed for Elstow in the hearth tax of 1671, 60 per cent had only one hearth and a further 20 per cent had two. The publicans and some of the farmers had three or four.

Then if we think that the Elstow manor house had 17 fireplaces, the Duncombes at Battlesden 13, the Brandreths at Houghton Regis 12 and the Caters at Kempston 22, we begin to get some idea of the comparatively small difference between life in the farm or the farm cottage and the very big difference between these and the small manor houses.

Statistically, there may appear to be an equally big difference between these manor houses and the over-large houses in which lived such people as the Duke of Bedford (Woburn) and the Earl of Ailesbury (Houghton House, Ampthill). However, in the first case the cottages and farmhouses varied as to whether all the necessary stages of food storage, processing, eating, living and sleeping took place in one room or seven; in this case it was more like the differences of today, more rooms for each function and a greater number and quality of possessions, plus of course rooms for servants.

Remains of Manor House at Elstow, once part of the nunnery. F9

Woburn Abbey 1987. Residence of the present Marquess of Tavistock, descendant of the 5th Earl of Bedford, who in 1694 became the 1st Duke. C14

Old Warden

An example of this 'middling' sort of house would be that designed for Robert Gostwick★, which he had adapted out of the old abbey buildings at Warden.

The inventory which was made seven or eight years after he acquired the lease in 1544 lists: two impressive reception rooms, five bedrooms, a kitchen fitted for cooking and a buttery fitted for brewing and bread making. The family rooms had heavy tapestries hanging on the walls, chairs, tables and chests all made and decorated by specialist joiners, tapestry and calf skin cushions and footstools covered with leather.

Robert Gostwick slept in a four-poster bed, with red and yellow curtains and with a red and yellow mat beside it. He had a cupboard for his clothes and a chest in which to keep his personal belongings. There was a fireplace in every room and extra rooms were added, so that by 1671 there were 20 heated rooms.

There were luxurious 'small' houses similar to this all over the county. When assessed in 1671 Oliver Luke's house at Cople Wood End had 27 hearths and Francis Dyve's house at Bromham 15. In addition to this there would have been unheated servants' rooms, work rooms and storage space.

Chicksands Priory and Someries, Luton

The Osborne house at Chicksands and the Crawley house at Someries, Luton (both 23 hearths) were assessed by the Parliamentary Sequestration Committee during the spring of 1644. We must not put too much reliance on these figures because we know that Lady Osborne was not living at Chicksands and had taken with her anything that she could quickly and easily convert into money for her husband's support. Also, that, although Lady Crawley did originally remain at Someries, her estates had been plundered and at one time troops were billetted round about. Nevertheless, it is of interest that Chicksands, which had been adapted from an old Priory c.1550 was definitely bigger, more ambitious but perhaps more old-fashioned.

At Chicksands, the hall, with its great log fire, sidetable (sideboard)

★Cousin of Sir John Gostwick of Willington.

Chicksands Priory 1987 – exterior. K11

Chicksands Priory 1987 – interior showing medieval tiled floor. K11

against the wall, long table, three round tables, two dozen chairs and a dozen stools stood ready to entertain a very large party. Sir John and his wife had five grown-up children, a resident chaplain and a nursery ready for the grandchildren.

At Someries, which was designed for Sir John Wenlock more than a century earlier and added to by Archbishop Rotherham, there was no mention of chapel or chaplain, although we know that the family were enthusiastic members of the established church and that part of their chapel still stands today. Undoubtedly, their chaplain would have accompanied Sir Francis and his son when they went to join the King and it may be that the parliamentary soldiers had removed what they considered 'superstitious' (holy) articles, leaving the room bare. The hall was used more in the modern sense and contained only two tables and forms. There was a dining room with the equivalent of a sideboard, a table with six chairs and six stools, although there were a dozen leather covered chairs in the great parlour.

There were six bedrooms, one of which was still referred to as the 'Queen's Chamber' commemorating the visit of King James I and Queen Anne in 1605, but like all the other rooms, the remaining furniture was plain and simple.

Six bedrooms at Someries, nine at Chicksands but when the assessors visited the house of Bedfordshire's most recently created Earl, who had recently died at Turvey, they found 22.

The Mordaunt House at Turvey

The first Earl of Peterborough had supported Parliament at Edgehill, but then took no further part in the fighting and died a few months later. His sons supported King Charles and so Parliament ordered that an inventory should be made of their mother's house.

'My ladyes Chamber a whit(e) wrought bed, 3 stooles, one Chaire, fire shovell and tongs and old hangings', £5.
'My lords chamber (Henry) 1 blew bed with the furniture, 3 litle Chaires, a Cubbard, fire shovell & tongs,' £1. 13. 0d.
'The servants chamber', 16 shillings.
'Mr Lewis Mordants Chamber...' his four-poster bed, 'haire coloured Curtaines', chaire, table, fire shovell and tongs, £1.
'His man's chamber', 10 shillings.

'Mistress Elizabeths Chamber...' her bed with red curtains, a cupboard, three low stools and two little tables, £1. 10s.
'The mayds Chamber one yellow bed', 10s.
'Mistress Margarets Chamber' a pallet bed, two chaires, a table, fire shovel and tongs, £1.
'Mr James' Chamber, 'a striped bed, a litle table & a Chaire', £2.

There were several more rooms including one for a servant to look after the children, one for the steward, an 'imbroyderer's chamber' and several others for servants and visitors. There were even beds in the 'Wainscott parlour' which may have been put up when they were mustering officers to go to war.

There was a hall, which may have served as the dining room, with two tables and four forms. A comfortable parlour, a drawing room with 18 stools, four chairs with woven seats, a table, a cupboard, fire irons in the big fireplace and two turkey work carpets. This room alone was valued at £10, the whole house at nearly £60.

The other five Bedfordshire Earls lived in even grander houses. In 1671 the Earl of Bolingbroke's house at Bletsoe had 38 hearths, the Cleveland house at Toddington had 45, Earl Grey's house, Wrest Park, had 52, the Earl of Ailesbury at Houghton House had 55 and Earl Russell's house at Woburn had 82!

Toddington Manor

Both the Earl of Wentworth and his son were ardent Royalists so the Parliamentary assessors also went to Toddington Manor in 1644. This grand house had been built in the mid-16th century by Lord Henry Cheney. Queen Elizabeth visited him in 1563, and her visit was commemorated by a suite of three rooms, 'The Queen's Suite', but the total value of their contents was only £1 because many things had been sold to cover the family's debts and others, especially articles of sentimental value, had been taken to London for safety.

Nevertheless, we can get a very good idea of what a really grand 17th century house was like.

In 1644 there were approximately 40 rooms; according to an old diagram they were arranged on three floors around a courtyard. The rooms were linked by a 'Green Gallery', 'Picture Gallery' and 'Wooden' or panelled gallery.

The dining-room table had a green baize cover and one of leather, the chairs and stools had matching woven seats; there was a fire place fitted for a large log fire. In the great parlour, there was a large, round, leather-covered table with two matching side tables and 17 matching chairs, a cupboard and another great fire place. There was a staff dining-room, a steward's room, bedrooms for the footmen, the nursery nurses, and in happier times, for the huntsman and the falconer. There were rooms for fencing, for playing billiards, and an indoor tennis court.

In the entrance hall was a table for playing 'shovell bord' and in a room next to the parlour, was a table covered in green leather with six matching chairs and six matching stools, which was probably a card room. Counting the servants' rooms there were more than 20 bedrooms. 'My Ladyes Chamber' had embroidered hangings on the wall, the four-poster bed had a 'vallence and Curtaines of old damaske' and a couch or daybed with a matching cover. There was a mattress and bolster, a cupboard, three stools, a little table and a chair beside the fire which had brass fire-dogs, fender and fire irons. The contents of this comfortable room was worth £5 and the 'little Ladyes Chamber' which had red curtains and vallence, a coverlet of 'old Holland' (tough cotton with a shiny surface) and a pallet bed with a matching coverlet for her maid to sleep on, a cupboard, and wicker chairs round the fire, were valued at £2. 10s. There were several other bedrooms of similar or higher value.

Charity begins at Home

Most 17th century villages of any size had at least one butcher, baker, grocer, shoemaker and possibly a tailor and a weaver. They mainly had a miller and at least one publican. There were usually men who could work with wood, metal and stone, so two or three villages together would be quite independent. Many of the country towns had a market, where goods or spare produce could be sold and the ladies could take homemade lace, or straw plait for hat making.

However, the rural economy was still very dependent on reasonable to good weather; there were few years when the harvest was good enough to make it possible to save money, for a 'rainy day'. The death of the father, unemployment, a fire, more than one lost harvest, were all examples of the disasters which could lead to destitution.

In 1563, a system of rates was devised so that small sums of money could be collected and paid out by the 'overseers of the poor' to relieve distress. In addition, collections could be taken in church and travellers sometimes left small, charitable sums in the towns where they stayed. Landowners often helped their own tenants and employees and many villages had their own charitable funds.

William Curtes of Elstow left sheep in the care of the church-wardens. They were to be hired out and the profits devoted to helping the poor. In 1571, John, the 2nd Lord Mordaunt, arranged for rents from land in Cardington to be used to support 'four poor almsfolk'.

Although few people could write, a surprising number could read their bibles.

By the time that Bunyan was five years old, several villages had a man or woman offering a simple form of education and there was the 'Harpur School' in Bedford and the 'Clerke School' at Houghton Conquest. Woburn School had been built by the Earl of Bedford as early as 1582 and there were one or two village schools. Thomas Whitehead, who owned a house on the green at Houghton Regis, arranged in 1654 for it to be converted into a school. This was during the Protectorate of Oliver Cromwell when the Established Church was not in favour. For this reason, although the original headmaster was the vicar of Totternhoe, the school was not restricted to children whose parents attended the parish church. In 1675, it combined with the National (Church of England) School. There was a school on the same site until 1967 when it moved to its present site; it is now known as The Thomas Whitehead Voluntary Aided Lower School.

Mordaunt family and other charities displayed in the porch of All Saint's Church, Turvey. C7

CHAPTER FIVE

An Unsettled Period

The young John Bunyan was probably sheltered from many of the troubles which hit Bedfordshire (and other counties) during the early years of his life. Reluctantly or otherwise, his family attended the parish church and do not appear to have been involved in the Laudian persecutions. However, no one could entirely avoid the effects of bad weather.

Despite the alarming rise of food prices in 1630 and 1631, following a period of bad weather which ended with the long wet winter and spring of 1629-30, rotting the seed corn in the ground and making it impossible to sow in the spring, Bunyan's family would have been partly protected from hunger. Although their low lying ground was very vulnerable, Thomas Bunyan's job as a brazier was comparatively well paid and, at times farmers would have paid him with food rather than with money. In towns such as Dunstable, where 20 people died in the plague outbreak of 1630, the poorer people may well have been suffering from malnutrition. Nor were the Bunyans personally troubled by the political unrest which was present in the county.

Local Politicians

As his father and grandfather walked the roads for miles around, calling at farms, inns and country houses, they would have heard talk that King Charles had summoned Parliaments in 1625, 1626 and 1628-29. No doubt they would have known that the Borough of Bedford was represented by the brother of the Earl of Bolingbroke (of

A Bolingbroke Family Monument in Bletsoe Church. E5

Bletsoe, Recorder of Bedford) Sir Beauchamp St John and the Earl's deputy and supporter, Richard Taylor of Clapham; also, that the county was represented by the Earl's son, Oliver Lord St John, and his cousin, Sir Oliver Luke, from Wood End, Cople. Whether they approved of this family's hold over the county we do not know, especially as other members of the Earl's family were local administrators.* During 1626–27 this tightly-knit group were reluctant to enforce the King's claims to receive financial gifts and enforced loans; a meeting was held at The Swan Hotel, Bedford in August 1626, at which the constables of North Bedfordshire voted against enforcing this disguised tax. Both Sir Beauchamp St John and Sir Oliver Luke spent some time in the Gatehouse Prison in London because of their refusal to pay.

To what extent these matters were discussed in the villages of Bedfordshire we cannot know, but the itinerant Bunyan family were

*Oliver 4th Lord St John was created Earl of Bolingbroke in 1624.

likely to have heard about them, especially when Parliament was dissolved in 1629 and the MPs returned home.

An Unpopular Tax

Politically, things went from bad to worse; the people of Elstow may not have been aware of the frustration felt by Bedfordshire's 20 or more JPs as the King and his advisers tried more and more to manipulate them and their offices but they were soon aware of his new policy for raising money. A committee of judges, including Sir Francis Crawley of Someries, Luton sat during 1634 and decided that, if the country was considered to be in danger, it was legal for the King to revive the ancient 'Ship Tax'.* In August 1635, at the end of Humphrey Monoux's year as sheriff (of Wootton) he was ordered to collect £3,000. It was his unwelcome duty to allocate that sum between the various districts of the county; local officials were to divide it up amongst individual towns and villages and then between all householders who were not considered to be in financial distress.

Richard Gery (of Bushmead) took over as sheriff a month later and between them they managed to collect all but £70 of the total. The following year, when Henry Chester (of Tilsworth) was sheriff, the inhabitants of Pulloxhill did what many other parishes must have talked of doing, they petitioned the Privy Council, complaining that there had been an unfair division of the tax.

Nevertheless, Henry Chester still managed to collect most of the money and his successor, William Boteler (of Biddenham) was only about £250 below target, much less than the deficit of some other counties.

William Plummer became sheriff, at the end of September 1638, just as the county hierarchy, officials, and the people of Bedfordshire mutually, or individually, decided to defy the law. So in 1639 Richard Childs (of Podington) was expected to enforce the comparatively small remaining debts of 1636 and 1637, the large sum still due from the previous year and his own target of £3,000! He called a meeting of his Constables and High Constables but the majority stayed away; of those who attended the meeting, very few agreed to collect the tax.

---

*The Ship Tax was originally levied from the maritime counties by Saxon Kings who wished to repel Danish ships.

Bushmead. The remains of the Priory, 1987. Once the home of the Sheriff, Richard Gery. N7

Biddenham Church, where the Boteler family are buried. E8

The people of Bedfordshire had been pushed too far; some who had previously refused to pay had been hounded unmercifully and those 'distressed' who were quite unable to pay, were assessed on their property. Such things as a horse at Tilbrook, a Bible at Risely, a chamber pot at Bletsoe, were among the many things seized.

The Bunyans and most of the people of Elstow appear to have paid their share, Elstow having had quite a low assessment.

Before King Charles called the 'Long Parliament' which brought the Ship Tax to an end, a new problem occurred which may have brought extra work to Thomas Bunyan II, the brazier.

Soldiers for Scotland

The feelings of King Charles for the Laudian Church were still very strong and in 1637 he tried to introduce Edward VI's Church of England Prayer Book into Scotland. The Scots resisted and the Lord Lieutenants were ordered to call out the county militia.

For some years militia service and practice had not been taken very seriously in Bedfordshire and, coupled with the local lack of enthusiasm for the policies of Bishop Laud, the Earl of Cleveland had the greatest difficulty in raising the 200 'trained' men who were expected of him.

The Scottish 'war' was a disaster; the English army was humiliated and by harvest time the reluctant soldiers were back home. The Bunyans would have heard many complaints from men who had been cheated of part of their pay. No doubt most of the soldiers told tales to anyone who would listen about their general dissatisfaction.

A Crisis of Government

Within a few years the residents of every town and village in the country would be discussing war. Not only in Bedfordshire but throughout the land, men had to argue with themselves as to whether their dislike of King Charles, his methods of ruling the country and/or his support of Archbishop Laud's 'papist' form of worship, would allow them to take up arms and fight against their 'King'. Meanwhile, Charles called Parliament together in 1640, sent them home after three weeks, only to recall them a few months later.

Sir Beauchamp St John again represented the Borough of Bedford but, as Mr Richard Taylor did not stand, the other seat went to Sir Samuel Luke, son of Sir Oliver. Thomas Lord Wentworth, son of one of the Lord Lieutenants (the other was Lord Grey of Wrest Park), won the other county seat in place of the Earl of Bolingbroke's son, Oliver Lord St John. However, Wentworth was soon summoned to join the Lords and a by-election was held. Sir Roger Burgoyne of Sutton, who had previously stood against Wentworth, on the next occasion stood against (the future Royalist) Sir Lewis Dyve of Bromham Hall, and this time he won.

As war broke out before the 'Long Parliament' was dissolved, three members remained in government while the Wentworths and Sir Lewis Dyve joined the king.

Sir Oliver Luke was on the committee which declared the Ship Money tax illegal and ordered the arrest of Archbishop Laud, who was sent to the tower. They set out to remove both the policies and the supporters of the Archbishop and were encouraged by a petition of support presented by 2000 people from Bedfordshire.

Between 1640 and 1660 freedom of worship swung further than many people could ever have dreamed possible; much further than many people thought desirable! John Bunyan was nearly 12 years old and a village boy preparing for his working, adult life when the members left Bedfordshire to sit in the 'Long Parliament'; he was 31, married, widowed, re-married father of children and had been preaching without any restriction for about five years by the time of the Restoration and the return of the strictly enforced 'established' church.

CHAPTER SIX

Civil War

On the 17 June 1642 the Commons ordered that Sir Beauchamp St John and Sir Oliver Luke should return home and organise the militia; this time for a cause which the people of Bedfordshire were sympathetic to.

Although Parliament was the first side to muster troops in the county, the Royalists soon showed their hand. Just over a month later, Sir Lewis Dyve rode into Bedford and ordered that 500 bullets should be made. On 26 July, messengers arrived at Bromham Hall bringing £1,000 so that Dyve could buy up all the available horses for use by the Royalist army.

An old doorway at Bromham Hall. E7

Bromham Hall 1987 with the River Ouse just across the lawn. E7

The following day, Sir Samuel Luke MP, the sheriff and some servants rode out to Bromham. They do not appear to have been expecting violence but their way was blocked by armed men. While the official party were waiting for reinforcements to be fetched from Bedford, Dyve escaped through the grounds, out of the county and went to join King Charles. Traditionally, he is said to have escaped by slipping out of the back door, crossing the lawn and swimming to the further bank of the River Ouse. Until recently, the thighboots which he is said to have left on the river bank were kept at the Hall.

When Dyve ordered the bullets he apparently referred to the opposition as 'Roundheads'. The well-known expressions 'Cavaliers' and 'Roundheads', spring from the days before the fighting began. One theory is that on the streets of London the rowdy apprentices and protesters who followed King Charles, shouting and jeering, tended to have close-cropped hair, 'round heads', while the young men from army families and Inns of Court, who formed his unofficial bodyguard, were known as 'Cavaliers'.

The causes which led to the outbreak of fighting, the various stages of military strategy and the actual battles have no place here. It is the

Bromham Bridge which at one stage in the Civil War was blocked by chains. E7

social changes which were forced on to the towns and villages of Bedfordshire and the effect on both the young John Bunyan and those numerous people in Bedfordshire and round about which concern us.

On 29 August 1642, King Charles raised his banner at Nottingham and war could no longer be prevented.

Although the people of Bedfordshire were mainly for Parliament, towns, villages and even families were divided by their loyalties. It is the names of the landed gentry that we know and quote, but we must remember that Sir Lewis Dyve would have expected all his tenants and estate workers to support him and any men not actually ill or disabled, to follow him to war. At a later stage in the war, some of his workers put chains and posts across the bridge at Bromham to delay Parliamentary soldiers who were passing through.

A Divided County

At Edgehill, the first battle of this tragic war, Dyve and his men of Bromham, the Earl of Cleveland, his men from Toddington and his

Wrest Park, now used by Silsoe College. (Until recently National Institute of Agricultural Engineering). 17th-century home of the Earl of Kent. H13

son, Thomas Lord Wentworth (who in 1656 raised the 1st Regiment of Guards now the Grenadier Guards), together with numerous smaller landowners and their men, fought on the side of King Charles. On the other hand, the Earl of Bedford, General of the Horse, and the Earl of Peterborough (from Turvey) General of the Ordnance fought for Parliament, beside the regiment raised by the Earl of Bolingbroke, who was the new Lord Lieutenant.* His son, Lord St John, and the son of the Earl of Kent from Wrest Park, commanded troops of horse, and Oliver, son of Oliver Cromwell was with them as a cornet (junior cavalry officer). Sir Samuel Luke was also commanding a troop of horse and was Scoutmaster General to the Earl of Essex. An even greater number of smaller landowners and their men lined up beside them.

No major battles were fought in Bedfordshire but nevertheless many men from all walks of life took part in the fighting and, although we will never know their names, some were killed and others returned home sick or seriously disabled.

*John, 5th Baron Mordaunt of Turvey, was created Earl of Peterborough in 1628. Henry, the 2nd Earl, who succeeded in 1643 was a supporter of King Charles.

At least 5,000 men were killed at Edgehill; the losses on both sides were frightening; some men, who had been ordered to fight were bitter and confused, others now had a loyalty to their fellows which counted as strongly as a loyalty to the cause. Some of the leaders came home in a state of shock; so much horror, so many deaths and nothing decided.

After Edgehill

The Earl of Bedford felt that the end of this first, disastrous battle, which neither side had won, could well be the opportunity to re-open peaceful negotiations. He rode to Oxford to discuss this with King Charles, Sir Francis Crawley and the King's other advisers but there was no way that they would agree to terms, which would be acceptable to Parliament. The Earl went home sadly, probably infuriated by both sides; he took no more part in the fighting and tried to remain neutral but from then on was suspected of having Royalist sympathies.

Lord St John died of wounds he received during the battle; his father was both sick and aged and their branch of the family also retired from further fighting. One or two other landowners also returned home and refused to fight again.

During December a petition was sent up to the House of Lords for transmission to the Commons, asking that negotiations should be opened with the King. Another was sent to the King, by 'divers of your Majesties Loyall Subjects inhabiting the County of Bedford amounting to the number of 3800' asking him to reopen negotiations with Parliament. Both failed.

No one consulted the wishes of the villagers; how did they feel when, as at Turvey, the 2nd Earl and his younger brother joined the Royalist army? A surprising number of families had one or more members fighting on each side.

Apart from the personal distress felt by the people of Bedfordshire, who had loved ones away with the army and the problem of making ends meet, as army pay of 7 pence (just under 3p) a day for a foot soldier was both low and invariably delayed, there was the difficulty of getting land ploughed, wheels mended and many other jobs done. As the years went by there were hardly any horses or carts left in the county, poor people were reduced to using breast ploughs and wheelbarrows and it was said that some farmers went out of business. The Parliamentary army made continual demands for food, money

*Memorial to the Mordaunt
family in All Saints Church,
Turvey.* C7

and supplies and as the years went by, and the soldiers were left unpaid
and hungry, there were continual thefts and raids by both sides.

Royalist Raids

In May 1643, all able-bodied men under 60 were ordered to report at
Leighton Buzzard. Most of the fighting during 1643 was in counties
south west and west of Bedfordshire but as soldiers were recruited or
pressed they were marched across the county. Some of these slipped
away and begged or stole food on their way back home.

The lonely widower, John Egerton, 1st Earl of Bridgewater, was
visiting his London house during June, having, so far, successfully
avoided committing himself to either side. His Ashridge estate was
raided by Royalist troops twice in ten days. Not only did they take
horses, plate and food supplies but also, in an attempt to find silver and
other valuables, 'beat down ceilings, heaved down the doors, though
open to them . . .'. They also went to the church, found the tomb of the
Earl's late wife and broke into it in search of jewellery or hidden plate.
To the Earl's distress they killed and carried off deer from the park, not

Ashridge House. Rebuilt during 1808–10 on the site of the original house adapted from a monastery. Now Ashridge Management College.

only males but '... does ready to fawn, and fawns that could hardly stand...'. The people of Bedfordshire were bound to suffer, having two main roads and several other important routes crossing the county. At Woburn there were complaints that both sides helped themselves to food as they passed through the village.

The War comes nearer Home

Although Parliament was in control of the county during October 1643, the Royalist, Sir Lewis Dyve, pressed local labour into making a garrison at Newport Pagnell and demanded money and provisions for its support. For a short time it looked as if he might take over North Bedfordshire. Early in the month his men surprised the county committee who were meeting at Ampthill, causing them to flee from the town. A week or two later he and his men were bold enough to enter Bedford and scatter the Parliamentary officers who were in the town recruiting. There was a scuffle on the bridge and for a short time, Dyve was in control of both the town and surrounding district.

Royalist sympathisers were able to hold a recruitment meeting at Shefford quite openly while some of Dyve's men were plundering the houses of Sir Samuel Luke at Cople and Sir John Burgoyne at Sutton. He had not forgotten the raid on Bromham Hall!

Wood End Farm, Cople, on the site of Sir Samuel Luke's Manor House. H9

Original moat of Wood End Farm while being cleaned out 1987. H9

Ampthill

Geographically, Ampthill was a suitable place for the (Parliamentary) county committee to meet, but politically, it was a strange choice. At Houghton House, Lord Elgin (father of Robert Lord Bruce), had at the outbreak of war, been preparing to join the King at Oxford when his wife persuaded him to remain at home rather than risk his life, wealth and their way of life in a war they were unlikely to win. Great Lodge, across the road, was rented by their distant relation, the widowed Margaret Nicolls, who had three sons serving in the Royalist army.

On the west side of Church Square lived Humphrey Iremonger supporter of Sir Lewis Dyve and with a son who became a quartermaster in the Royalist army. So strong was the Royalist support in the town that in 1646 someone painted the badge of the Prince of Wales on a wall of the inn now known as the 'White Hart'.

News of these skirmishes would have soon reached Elstow and, no doubt, the 15-year-old John Bunyan and his friends would have found it very exciting. The Bunyans, travelling from house to house would have been met by people asking for news of all these events and we can imagine the talk, the gossip, the eye-witness accounts and the exaggerations!

Park House, Ampthill – Rebuilt in 1694. E/F12

Coat of Arms of the Prince of
Wales, painted in the White
Hart, Ampthill in 1646. E/F12

Georgian front to the 17th century 'Red Hart', Ampthill. (Now White
Hart). E/F12

The Defence of Bedfordshire

Before the attack on Bedford, recruitment had been increasingly difficult. The people left in towns and villages were discouraged and had lost any will they had to fight. It became obvious to the parliamentary officers that either the royal garrison at Newport Pagnell must be driven out or Bedfordshire would be lost.

The Earl of Essex was at St Albans and sent a large detachment of soldiers on ahead to Dunstable. The newspaper, 'A Perfect Diurnall', reported '... that they had most cruelly plundered Bedfordshire in divers places, and the day past came to Dunstable in that County, where was a great Faire kept that day, and made great spoile there.' Another paper, blamed the inhabitants of Bedford and Dunstable for inviting them into the towns.*

These soldiers, together with reinforcements sent from London, continued on to Newport Pagnell. They were so successful that during the night of 26 October, Dyve and his soldiers marched out to Stony Stratford, without waiting to defend the site.

Soon afterwards, Sir Samuel Luke became the new governor on behalf of Parliament and from then on the people of Bedfordshire were under even more strain as the civilians were forced to offer their manual labour.

The Raids Continue

There was a small, defensive garrison at Bedford on the site of the old castle keep. The Earl of Essex felt that this was unnecessary once the Newport Pagnell garrison had been completed. The County Committee strongly disagreed, especially when, during June 1644, groups of Royalist soldiers raided south-west Bedfordshire.

One of the best reported incidents appeared in the Parliamentary news sheet, dated Monday 24 June 1644. Information had been received that the King's forces were continually raiding Bedfordshire, Buckinghamshire and Hertfordshire '... committing many great and cruell outrages ...'.

On the previous Sunday, the King had passed through Hockley in

---

*There are no October fairs recorded for Dunstable.

the Hole (Hockliffe) on the way to Bedford and his soldiers had

> ... plundered Leighton, and sent another party to Dunstable, where they entered the Towne when the people were at Church, not contenting themselves with plunder, but made a great disturbance, cutting and slashing the people in the [Priory] Church, and shot a case of Pistols at the Minister in the Pulpit, but missed him; and afterwards abused him very inhumanely. The like outrage they committed as divers Townes and Villages thereabouts, and at Woodborne [Woburn] the Earle of Bedfords house. They also faced Newport Pannell, but Sir Samuel Luke let fly 2 or 3 of his great peeces which set them packing.*

The 'Earle's House' may be a reference to the occasion when Birchmore House on the Woburn estate was raided. The attack on the garrison at Newport Pagnell was carried out by the Earl of Cleveland with his brigade of horse. He was driven off by Luke's heavy guns.

While they were in Dunstable, the Royalist soldiers had commandeered horses from the Red Lion on the corner of Church Street. The wealthy innkeeper, John Plott, came out himself to explain that his business could not continue without post horses. He was shot dead as he stood there arguing.

The King himself was as near as Hockliffe; it is said that on this or some other occasion he stayed at Ascott House, Wing, and that during his visit one of his soldiers stole a silver chalice from the village church. Charles sent for him, heard the evidence and ordered his execution at Wing crossroads.

The Garrison at Newport Pagnell

The Bedford garrison was allowed to remain and in September 1644 men from Carlton, Colmworth and Eaton Socon were ordered to come into Bedford and carry out any necessary repairs.

Meanwhile, at Newport Pagnell, Luke was so short of food and money that his unpaid and ill-fed soldiers were looking for chances to desert. Smallpox broke out and Oliver, son of Oliver Cromwell, was amongst those who died.

Luke's work was never-ending; not only must he defend the area

---

*The modern style 's' is used in this quotation.

but he often received orders to meet arms, men and money at Dunstable or Bedford and escort them to their next stage north. Despite his own shortage of supplies he must feed and provide uniforms for recruits, watch out for escaping men who had been conscripted, act as area commander, keep accounts, answer correspondence and liaise with all the local committees, national committees, and the Parliamentary leaders. He wrote letter after letter to the County Committee, begging for men, money and supplies. He was helped with these jobs by many local men, including his muster master, Henry Whitbread, and his treasurer, the Rev. Edward Harrison of Kensworth, who not only handled the money but acted as a private messenger and 'diplomat'.

It is more than likely that it is at this garrison that Bunyan spent most of his military service.

CHAPTER SEVEN

John Bunyan becomes a Soldier

Being so near Bedford, Elstow must have suffered badly, especially as
the village lay beside a main road. If Thomas Bunyan had failed to
volunteer for military service he probably would have been too old for
conscription. He was in his early forties, a skilled brazier and as far as
we know a perfectly healthy man. It may be that his itinerant work
gave him the opportunity to get advance news of when the muster
soldiers were coming and the opportunity to keep out of the way. It is
also likely that the landowners would have conspired to keep such a
useful man out of the army.

A 'Thomas Bunyan' has been found amongst a list of soldiers
fighting for the King but it was a common name and there is no
evidence to suggest that he came from Elstow. Although we have no
evidence either way, it is, of course, possible that as a civilian he took a
regular turn of maintenance work at Newport Pagnell.

John was 16 in November 1644 and he must have been working with
his father, at least part-time, for some years. Even had he wanted to
avoid military service, it is doubtful if he could have escaped much
longer.

By 1642, when the men of Bedfordshire and other parts of England
met each other in battle at Edgehill, John was nearly 14. Most of the
landlords and as far as we know, most of the villagers of Bedfordshire,
were supporting Parliament but at Elstow Sir Thomas Hillersden
supported King Charles as did another of the local landowners, John
Kidd.

The roads became dangerous and roadside farms and houses were at
risk. It may be that livestock and household stores were safer at
Harrowden than at Elstow.

Thomas Bunyan I, the chapman, died twelve months before the
battle but Thomas II and John continued to travel around making

The north door, Elstow church. F9

small repairs and bringing larger jobs home to make or mend in the workshop.

A skilled metal worker found travelling along the roads would have risked being pressed into the army and, if John was well away from home and friends, his youth would not necessarily have saved him. However, he would have known every greenway and footpath for miles around and would have kept out of the way of marching or camped soldiers. If in 1642 the family owned a horse and cart it would soon have been commandeered or stolen but nevertheless as supplies became more and more difficult to come by, father and son would have been busier than ever before, repairing old tools and kitchen utensils.

Once Parliament had complete control over Bedfordshire and garrisons were built at Bedford and Newport Pagnell, they would have had to take a share in maintenance work. John may well have enjoyed the break from routine and the opportunity to meet soldiers from all over the country. As a skilled metal worker, he would have been treated with respect which would be very pleasant for a country boy.

John loses his Mother and Sister

During the spring of 1644 there was a serious outbreak of smallpox at the Newport Pagnell garrison in which several soldiers died, including

Oliver, son of Oliver Cromwell. With so many men crowded into unhygienic camps, and the continual stream of unpaid, sick and wounded soldiers travelling the roads, quite small villages suffered outbreaks of the summer plague and other illnesses. In a normal summer one or, at the most, two people would be buried in Elstow churchyard but in July 1644, there were seven and in August, another five.

One of the first was John's mother, 40-year-old Margaret Bunyan and one of the last, his 14-year-old sister. One cannot doubt the shock this would be to a 15-year-old boy, however grown up and experienced he was. Also, however good his relationship with his father, and whatever was the custom of the neighbourhood, he must have been extremely resentful when only a few weeks later his father married for the third time and brought another lady into their household.

John Bunyan joins the Army

John was not 16, the legal age at which a man could be impressed, until 30 November.

Following a disastrous recruitment attempt in 1643, Sir Samuel Luke was desperate for men at the Newport Pagnell garrison and in 1644 Parliament ordered Bedfordshire to supply 225 men. A large party was impressed by the end of November and it seems likely that the young John Bunyan was among them.

Quite apart from the horrors of the actual fighting, military service in any century has a very great effect upon a young man. It removes them from the community in which they have grown up, which in the case of a 17th-century village was almost like an extended family, and puts them down to find their own level amongst men from different parts of the country, from different social backgrounds and, above all, of different levels of experience of life and education.

We can assume that amongst the men that Bunyan met at Newport Pagnell were the shy and timid, the extrovert and braggards, the quiet and studious, the quiet and simple, the noisy loud-mouthed know-alls boasting of their sexual conquests, their bravery and the clever trickery by which they escaped from everything unpleasant be it an enraged father or a deserted girl, an unwanted military duty or an officer accusing them of negligence.

It seems unlikely that he was billetted there for less than two-and-a-half years; during that time surely he must have found companions who shared his love of the countryside and his problems of understanding what life was all about. As with all the points that interest us about his life, we are left searching through his books looking for clues about his experiences and we find very few indeed.

Education at Newport Pagnell

One fact we cannot escape from is that the boy who claimed to have had very little education and had little pleasure from it* and to have quickly forgotten most of what he had learned, could at the age of 28 write a booklet, *Some Gospel – Truths Opened*, and go on to write well over 50 more books, pamphlets and essays. Millions of words, all painfully handwritten; even if we forget the sheer physical effort, from where did he get the vocabulary?

His spelling, although not perfect, is under the circumstances quite amazing. Depending on his subject he used varying amounts of biblical words and phrases and if he had limited his writing to biblical arguments and language his books would not be so surprising. As, however, he became more confident he wrote about all manner of subjects, bringing in all his accumulated experience; places he had visited, people he had met and above all, spiritual debate that he had struggled with over the years. It is because, in his more popular works, that his characters use the simple conversational remarks and arguments of his less educated companions rather than those of his preachers and teachers that we find them readable to this day.

This is not the place for a long essay about the educational facilities at Newport Pagnell. Many village boys, frustrated by the restrictions of the education offered at their local school, returned home from the two World Wars of the twentieth century able for the first time in their lives to enjoy reading, even if they still found writing a bit of a struggle.

Sir Samuel Luke

The Commander at Newport Pagnell was Sir Samuel Luke, a responsible and respected soldier and an educated man. His numerous

---

*Although this may be because the books used added to his religious and social turmoil.

surviving letters show him to have wide interests and to be far from narrow in his outlook and enjoyment of life. Until these letters became better known, his reputation was marred by a book written by his personal secretary, Samuel Butler.

Unlike Luke, Samuel Butler's 'hero', Hudibras, was a strict, narrow-minded military commander, a presbyterian with short hair and plain, dark clothes but in his satire he gives Hudibras characteristics that he observed when they were working together at Cople End. There is no evidence that Luke even knew John Bunyan as an individual soldier, although his father, Sir Oliver Luke, had a personal servant called Edward Bunyan. As Cople is so near Harrowden, this could well be John's uncle, so it is just possible that Luke did at least know him by sight.

The soldiers in the garrison were very mixed, many of them uneducated. Some were skilled craftsmen or husbandmen who had been conscripted and were watching for any attempt to escape and get back home, others were petty criminals, thieves and highway robbers who were looking for a chance to carry on their 'trade' both within the garrison and outside.

So Luke was obliged to have very strict discipline, keep his men fully occupied and in an attempt to make them better soldiers and better men, try to educate them so that they understood the reason for fighting, and what were the ideas and changes that a successful Parliamentarian party would try and bring about.

Vera Brittain, in her book *In The Steps of John Bunyan*, suggests that he 'presided over his resentful collection of country bumpkins like a Presbyterian Baden-Powell'! Certainly, in a desperate attempt to discipline the untrained and unwilling men that were sent him to defend the garrison, he worked on the principal of keeping them busy throughout their waking hours and tried to prevent them leaving the camp to go into the town.

Presbyterian and Independent Preachers at Newport Pagnell

We know that two books had been especially mass produced for the use of soldiers, *The Souldiers' Pocket Bible* and *The Souldiers' Catechism* and that they were freely handed out to any who could make use of them. In addition, there were news-sheets printed by both armies as quoted in Chapter 6 and pamphlets put out to support

various religious and political points of view. There was even light
reading in the form of ballad sheets. When Bunyan arrived at Newport
Pagnell there were seven officially appointed Presbyterian chaplains;
there were regular services and two sermons were preached each
Sunday and one on Thursdays. Each day started with prayers and a
Bible reading and there were often lectures and study periods in the
evenings, there were great opportunities for education.

What the teenage boy, who already had such spiritual problems,
would have found interesting were those informal evening 'lectures'
which, rather in the manner of those courses today organised by the
Workers' Education Association, were part instruction and part
discussion.

Amongst the seven chaplains was William Dell, an inspired
preacher who was rector of Yeldon. Although it is unlikely that he got
to know John Bunyan the soldier, he would later support him as a
preacher and invite him into his own church.

One life-long friend who Bunyan possibly did meet for the first time
while he was still at Newport Pagnell, was the young John Gibbs, who
in 1646 became vicar of Newport Pagnell and in the following year,
vicar of St Peter and St Paul, Bedford. They may even have known
each other before the war, because Gibbs was only 18 months older
than John and was the son of a Bedford cooper. He had been to Sidney
Sussex College, Cambridge, where he must have been used to hearing
all views of opinion discussed.

Some people even doubt if Bunyan was ever at Newport Pagnell,
because when he returned home his spiritual problems were not eased
by discussion but were even worse. We must, however, remember the
severity of the Presbyterian form of Christianity and to quote Mrs
Brittain again: 'For nearly three years, John Bunyan lived in a religious
atmosphere, created by the standards of the Old Testament.'

Although we know that there were Independents throughout the
Parliamentary army and several at Newport Pagnell, they were
disapproved of by many of the officers and men and ministers like the
Rev. Edward Harrison of Kensworth, who had accepted the idea of
adult baptism, did not become chaplains until after the garrison at
Newport Pagnell had been dismantled.

Another Form of Education?

Another feature of garrison life, which may in retrospect have added to

Bunyan's spiritual and emotional problems, was the opportunity for slipping out and drinking and mixing with the ladies, who had been attracted to the town by the presence of the garrison. There was a strict rule that the men should be back in barracks by 9.00 p.m. but, as with any situation where men are kept under these conditions, there are ways and means! It seems likely that he and his friends could and did slip away from these religious and political discussions and behaved in a way that they would not have done at home.

CHAPTER EIGHT

Another Battle

The months leading up to the Battle of Naseby put further strain on the people of Bedfordshire. Although, following a petition to Parliament, one detachment of soldier was moved out of the county during March 1645, thefts and 'free quartering' (an obligation on local people to support soldiers who were resting or in training), continued. The Earls of Bolingbroke and Elgin* (Bletsoe and Houghton House) estimated that these outrages had added £50,000 pounds to the official payments extracted from the county. Robberies by unpaid and ill-fed soldiers made country life even more difficult; farms and cottages in isolated hamlets such as Harrowden must have been continually at risk.

More quartered soldiers were moved out of the county in May and the men meeting in the alehouses or working in the fields must have discussed if and when the next battle would come. After the long, miserable winter they must have looked forward to a major battle, outside the county of course, which would hopefully decide, once and for all, the relationship between King and Parliament. Then the local men would come home, the strangers go away, and as soon as possible things would return to normal.

When Oliver Cromwell and his cavalry rode into Bedford on 11 June, many people must have come out to greet them, ask questions and even stand them drinks in an effort to get news of friends and families. Luke, in a letter to his father, suggested that at times the soldiers made up for the shortage of bread by imbibing extra beer!

In 1645, Parliamentary soldiers surprised the Royalist, Sir Charles

---

*In 1633, Lord Bruce was created Earl of Elgin by King James I. Following the Restoration, King Charles II rewarded the 2nd Earl with the English title, Earl of Ailesbury.

Campton Manor House. K12

Bullet holes at Campton House where the owner, Sir Charles Ventris was surprised in 1645 by Parliamentary soldiers but escaped. K12 Right: *The religious figures painted on the screen of Roxton Church had their faces removed by Parliamentary soldiers, who stabled their horses in the church.* L6

Ventris, when he returned to his house at Campton. He escaped but bullet holes are carefully preserved in the house.

The soldiers of Oliver Cromwell have been blamed for damage in many English churches but they were mainly devout Christians. They just destroyed anything which they connected with the Roman Catholic Church, such as the painted screen in Roxton Church. They removed the faces and according to legend, stabled their horses in the church.

Six hundred men and nearly as many horses camped overnight and marched out at 6.00 a.m. next morning. They joined a delighted Sir Thomas Fairfax in time to prepare for the forthcoming battle. Two days after they left Bedford they were fighting at Naseby in Northamptonshire and, surprisingly soon, they had at last won their complete victory.

Men and Supplies Needed

King Charles escaped towards the Welsh border and the Parliamentary army spent some months gaining control of various Royalist strongholds.

The people of Bedford could see that they were still at risk and were horrified when on 3 July men arrived in the town prepared to dismantle the garrison. Sir Thomas Alston, of Odell, had arrived in time to order them to leave it alone but they could easily return, so men from Bedford and the surrounding countryside presented a petition, stating that they considered themselves to be in great danger and begging for the 'fort' to remain. In support of their argument, they pointed out that on the very next day that the men came to destroy the garrison, only ten miles away at Fenny Stratford Royalist soldiers robbed '... divers, Carriers and Passengers coming to the Fair at Woolborne'. Although they were proved correct, their petition failed; a few days later the fort was dismantled, and the town was asked to pay the bill for work which left the town undefended!

On another occasion in the same year, soldiers who were behaving badly at Elstow Fair were chased off by the local people.

On Monday, 25 August, the day that Oliver Cromwell signed an 'engagement of safety to the citizens of Bristol', King Charles passed through Bedfordshire on his way back to Oxford. Three hundred soldiers gathered on the riverside meadows of Great Barford and plundered Goldington. Lieut. Col. Richard Cockayne, who had served at Newport Pagnell, tried to prevent them but the approach of King Charles with a larger troop of horses forced him to retreat into Bedford. The next morning Charles led his soldiers into the town. The garrison had left but Cockayne gathered such men as he could and fought the Royalist soldiers on Bedford bridge.

South of the County

Nevertheless, Charles rode on into Woburn; he probably passed the night at the Abbey while his troops camped round about. They stayed there long enough to gather supplies for their journey before moving on to Dunstable. Charles rested at the Red Lion while, no doubt, his soldiers were once more helping themselves to food and drink before continuing along the Icknield Way. Stragglers who did not arrive until the next morning, formed themselves into an official-looking troop and rode into Luton where they demanded £250 in the name of the King. (To get some idea of the sum involved, the horse troopers were supposed to receive two shillings per day.) It would obviously take time to collect such a large sum so the soldiers were prepared to wait. Parliamentary soldiers were passing through Markyate and messengers from Luton managed to fetch them in time. They rode into the town, caught the Royalists off their guard and managed to kill four of them and capture 22 men and horses before the rest were driven out of the town.

Leighton Buzzard had several times had cause to complain about the number of Parliamentary soldiers they were expected to support. In November, while King Charles was still at Oxford, Royalist troops were out foraging along the Bedfordshire-Buckinghamshire borders. They spent the night of the 26th at Leighton Buzzard and, according to the parliamentary news sheet, they then rode out towards Woburn. Four young and possibly reckless young men rode out to meet them and fired shots before turning and riding back into the town. The soldiers followed them but before they could start collecting food or looking for horses, they were attacked by the people of Woburn. Of course, they rode quickly away and came back with many more soldiers. This gave the townspeople time to call others in from the surrounding villages and to get together an assortment of arms. They stood firm and resisted the raiders until they succeeded in killing the Royalist major. From then on the soldiers were completely out of control and set fire to more than one house.

When they eventually rode away, fire was raging right down one side of the street; houses were not only robbed of all food and valuables but wantonly damaged.

A few weeks later, 28 residents sent a petition to the House of Lords describing the numerous raids that they suffered. They claimed that on this last raid, 17 or 18 houses were destroyed, as well as stables and

Sealed Knot staging a mock battle on Elstow Green, 1985. By kind permission of the Rev. J. Tibbs. F9

outhouses. Several people had lost their livelihood; inns and malt houses had been burnt. Several families had been left homeless and others had lost food, clothes and their working stock. The House of Lords granted their petition that they might be allowed to 'have a collection in London, Westminster and the Associated Counties for the relief of their distress'.

Even with Charles practically confined at Oxford and his army in ruins, still the ill-feeling and occasional fighting occurred. In January 1646, the county was still suffering from the demands of horse troopers wintering on their farms and in February yet another 150 men were conscripted and sent to Newport Pagnell.

CHAPTER NINE

Religious Upheaval

During the years following his return to Elstow, after, but not apparently immediately after, his time in the army, the young John Bunyan lived through many painful years of religious trauma.

He became a willing member of the Elstow church, where Christopher Hall appears to have been ignoring the ban on surplices and ceremony, only to decide that the reason for his enjoyment of the church was suspect if not blasphemous. John Bunyan's behaviour, which would probably have been quite acceptable in 1988, his love of games and bell-ringing which we would consider commendable, his love of what was probably by today's standards middle-of-the-road, Anglican services, together with the double standards that he saw all around him, sent him off onto a personal religious pilgrimage which drove him to the edge of sanity.

The confusion and distress that John Bunyan suffered and which led to his position as a popular (in the best sense of the word) preacher and his books, especially *The Pilgrim's Progress* and *Mr Badman*, were greatly aggravated by the situation in mid-17th century Bedfordshire.

A Petition to Parliament

It was late in the year 1640 that the duly elected Members of Parliament rode off to Westminster to attempt to resolve the religious and economic problems that had caused such distress in Bedfordshire.

How quickly they succeeded can be illustrated by the petition which was delivered to Parliament on 16 March of the following year. An apparently endless stream of riders passed through Elstow and were joined by others on their journey so that by the time that they reached

Finsbury Fields there were about two thousand of them. Having rested, they lined up into a column, four abreast and, led by the High Sheriff, rode to Westminster where Sir John Burgoyne presented their petition to the House of Commons.

They thanked Parliament for removing the 'superstitious innovations' (of Archbishop Laud), the removal of illegal taxes (the Ship Tax), the abolition of the Star Chamber (where Edward Alport had summoned the people of Dunstable) and the Court of High Commission, which had been responsible for driving out Peter Bulkley and Zachary Symmes.

They then went on to ask for the removal of all evil councillors and the 'complete removal of all burdensome and scandalous ceremonies, and of all corrupt and scandalous ministers'. They wanted Parliament to provide and maintain 'learned, pious, and conscientious' ministers 'especially in market towns and populous places'.

Finally, those 'pious and painful divines' who had been deprived of their livings 'might receive ample reparation'.

This petition was greatly appreciated by Parliament and, as seen above, once the Civil War broke out Parliament quickly took control of this area and the ideas that Archbishop Laud had tried to force onto local churches became illegal. Altar rails, stained glass windows, 'images' and statues were all removed. Special surplices and ceremony were forbidden, all forms of work and entertainment on Sundays were made illegal.

Puritan Rule

As the control of Parliament became stronger so the 'Puritan' faction could work openly. In 1643 an Act was passed whereby clergy would no longer be ordained by a bishop but be appointed by a committee. In 1645 it became illegal to use the Book of Common Prayer which was replaced by a 'Directory of Public Worship'.

To swear in such a way as to take the name of God in vain, became classed as a serious sin and to act in plays, dance or make music was in the eyes of many puritans an offence against God.

John Bunyan was only 15 years old in 1643 so he never really knew any other religious climate. His childish nightmares, his adult worries and his final weeks of despair all took place against this strict Puritan background.

The Loss of a Living

The request for 'learned, pious and conscientious ministers' led to many changes: out went Giles Thorne of St Mary's and St Cuthbert's, John Bradshaw of St Paul's and Theodore Crowley of St John's, all of Bedford, John Goodwin of Leighton Buzzard, John Birde of Luton and William Peddar of Dunstable.

For a variety of reasons, many village clergy also lost their livings, e.g. Nathaniel Hill of Renhold was driven out because he was away with the Royalist army, John Ailmer of Melchbourne because he was a 'common drunkard', Edward Marten of Houghton Conquest, for 'papistical innovations' such as bowing five times before the altar each time he went up or down the steps. But Christopher Hall, vicar of Elstow, managed to satisfy the critics.

John Syddall of Kensworth appears to have been one of the ministers who was forced to leave because he could not come to terms with the new informal form of service. There was an accusation, unproven, that he was a 'frequenter of alehouses' but the committee probably took more seriously the fact that he refused to administer communion to anyone who would not come up to the rails to receive it. Later, when the rails were taken down, he said that this act was '. . . the beginning of the abomination of desolation . . .' and, very revealing of his real problems, that 'whoremongers and drunkards are as excusable as those that go from their own parish to hear sermons' and he said that 'Papists were better subjects than Puritans'.

In their wisdom the committee appointed in his place Edward Harrison, a recently ordained minister from Kent.

For many years, the events described had been a bitterly fought stuggle between the strict, maybe 'High' Church of England and the Puritan reformers who were fighting for varying degrees of change within the established church. Some of these wanting and eventually obtaining, freedom from episcopal control, that is, ordination by bishops.

The 'Independents'

Several of the new intake of clergy were to go even further and speak out against the 'Presbyterian committee' form of church government as being no better than one based on bishops and archbishops. William

Dell, the new Rector of Yeldon, who became a chaplain in the Parliamentary army, both preached and wrote that if one set of 'lords' (bishops) were removed and replaced with another set (committee officials) the church would still swarm with ruling lords who would between them, hide '... Christ's own lordship and dominion'.

Early Baptist Preachers

Phillip Goodwin, the man appointed as lecturer at Hemel Hempstead in 1641, was still in the area and when the Vicar of St Mary's was removed, his replacement, George Kendall, invited him into the church to preach. They caused a great scandal and spent a short time in prison because they both believed that only people who had made the deliberate commitment of adult baptism should be admitted to full church membership.

Before they were arrested and removed from the parish, Edward Harrison had visited Hemel Hempstead and had come round to their way of thinking. He resigned from the living at St Mary's Kensworth but bought a cottage and apart from his spell in the army remained at Kensworth for some years.

The Independents were greatly disliked by the Presbyterian members of Parliament and by most of the Presbyterian military commanders, including Samuel Luke at Newport Pagnell. Nevertheless, there were several such lecturers preaching unofficially 'on the fringe' at Newport Pagnell and John Bunyan must have been aware of the wide spectrum of belief in the villages around him.

Carlton Baptist Church, connected with the Bunyan family. C5

CHAPTER TEN

John Bunyan's First Marriage

On the 6 August 1646, Parliament ordered that the garrison should at last be demolished and many of the men returned home during the autumn. By this time Parliament was concerned to help the Protestants in Ireland and it was decided to send some of the soldiers from Newport Pagnell to Chester to await further orders before marching them on to the coast. Not all the soldiers wanted to go and volunteers were called for.

John obviously decided that he was in no hurry to return home and that to travel to Ireland would be an opportunity to see more of life. A 'John Bunyan', who was probably the author, accompanied a Captain O'Hara as far as Chester and back again to Newport Pagnell without apparently having had the chance to cross the sea although in *Grace Abounding* he mentions amongst a list of his adventures that on one occasion he '... fell into a creak of the sea, and hardly escaped drowning'.

It is generally considered that he was among those men who were sent home from Newport Pagnell the week after Cromwell brought his army to Bedford, so that he and the other commanders could negotiate with King Charles who was lodged at Woburn. Negotations continued but fighting broke out again, there were more taxes, more soldiers to be quartered and fed, more defeated and unpaid soldiers trying to find their way home across Bedfordshire and Hertfordshire but John Bunyan's war was over. He returned home, presumably to the cottage at Harrowden although he could have stayed with friends or with 'grandmother' Bunyan at the cottage by the Green.

In the museum which is run by the Bunyan Meeting House at Bedford is an anvil with 'J. BVNYAN' carved on one side and '1647 HELSTOWE' on the other. He must have decided to go back to his life as a metal worker, either using the family forge or perhaps deciding

Bunyan's Anvil. Now in the Bunyan Museum, Bedford.

to keep away from Harrowden and make his living by walking the roads and doing repairs where he found them.

Married Life

Another important fact for which we have no written records is the first marriage of John Bunyan. Civil marriage was not instituted until 1653 and during the Civil War the parish registers were not properly filled in. The birth of his first daughter, Mary, is entered at Elstow on 20 July 1650, so we can assume that he married some time after he was settled back in the village. We assume that the baby took her mother's name of 'Mary' but we do not know. It appears that Christopher Hall, the vicar, conscientiously kept the parish registers up-to-date until he was obliged to hand them over to William Cass, on the 21 December 1653* and, as we know that Bunyan's wife was a godly lady, had they been married at Elstow the entry would undoubtedly have been recorded.

It may well be that she came from the Newport Pagnell area; he could even have married her at the time that he was preparing to leave the garrison and brought her back to Elstow with him. We have seen that the few personal remarks that he included in *Grace Abounding* are

*He had been elected by the people of Elstow and was respected by Christopher Hall, as, 'an able and honest man'.

not always intended to be taken as accurate pieces of biography but when he records that he and his young wife were, 'as poor as poor might be, not having so much household stuff as a dish or spoon betwixt us both,...' it seems as though they either started their married life in the family home at Harrowden or as lodgers elsewhere. No doubt they moved into their High Street cottage, thought to be on the site of the St Helena Restaurant, when they had managed to make and buy a few essential pieces of furniture.

After recording his marriage, the next few paragraphs of *Grace Abounding* appear to record in the correct order, a series of events which became gradually more distressing until they led to an emotional breakdown. His wife had brought to Elstow two books which had been bequeathed to her by her late father. One, *The Practice of Piety*, a small book of meditations published in 1612, is in part unbelievably gruesome.

It is dreadful to think of someone who suffered from the morbid introspection that Bunyan had previously recorded, reading a piece written to illustrate the miseries of a man about to die but who had not been 'reconciled to God in Christ'. A man who reached such a state of terror that '... the face waxeth pale, the nose blacke, the nether jaw-bone hangeth down, the eye-strings break, the tongue faltreth...'!

However at this period of his spiritual life, these works did not seem to distress him.

The other book, *The Plain Man's Pathway to Heaven* published by Arthur Dent, in 1601, also dealt with what he would regard as morbid subjects, such as sin, salvation and damnation. However, a young man, would find this book easier to read because the arguments put forward were discussed by four 'Interlocutors, a divine, an honest man, an ignorant man and a caviller'.

Bunyan records that he and his wife would sit and read these two books and that although he found them interesting, they did not bother him and that he did not identify with the miserable sinners in the stories. Perhaps his years as a soldier had put a defensive skin around his tender conscience.

He gives us no inkling that his wife was distressed by his behaviour and one wonders if by the standards of today his behaviour was so very bad. However, she did tell him what a godly man her father had been and what a good life he had led and how he had encouraged others to do the same.

*The house in Elstow High Street where John Bunyan once lived (date unknown).
By kind permission of Bedfordshire County Council.* F9

Churchgoing

Although these books did not depress Bunyan, they did make him
think and being also influenced by his wife, he began to attend church
twice each Sunday. Rather to his surprise, he found that he quite
enjoyed it.

The Rev. Christopher Hall came to Elstow during the period when
Archbishop Laud was persecuting the Presbyterian ministers of
Bedfordshire (see above) and presumably conformed. Although he
adopted some of the Puritan ideals, such as discouraging games on
Sundays, he somehow managed to continue using the Common
Prayer Book services which Bunyan came to enjoy.

So, assuming that Bunyan did not rearrange events in *Grace*

Abounding in order to make his spiritual progress more easy to follow, some time around 1650, despite the orders from Parliament that only 'Presbyterian', non-prayer book services should be held, he was able to appreciate 'all things (the high-place, priest, clerk, vestment, service and what else) belonging to the church', in other words, the 'symbols' and the ritual which Parliament deplored.

He enjoyed taking part in the familiar responses, and the feeling of being one with the rest of the community, but above all he enjoyed ringing the church bells.

Troubled by a Sermon

Looking back ten to fifteen years, Bunyan is quite sure that at that period of his life he was not bothered by a sense of sin and that once work or church was over and the chores around the cottage finished he would join up with those companions of his youth and once more play games upon the village green. Possibly on Sundays, they tried to confine their more rowdy games away from the road and cottages and not call too much attention to themselves but, as such games involving a lot of people usually do, they gradually got noisier and more publicly intrusive until in the end, one Sunday morning, Christopher Hall got up in the pulpit and preached a powerful sermon on the evil of breaking the sabbath, either with 'labour, sports or otherwise'.

The young man, who ten or more years before had trembled at a similar sermon, awoke once again to the knowledge of his great sin. Hall was he knew speaking directly to him. The moment the sermon ended he hurried out of the church and went home with a great burden on his spirit.

He walked home, went in through the familiar door, sat down to the dinner that his wife had prepared for him, dozed in his familiar chair and found that he could almost feel the weight of his guilt slipping away from him. How relieved he must have been when Hall's words began to fade; 'the fire was put out' and he knew that he could sin again without this unbearable weight of sin.

He hurried back to the Green and joined his friends in a game of tip-cat, in which it was necessary to tip the cat (a piece of wood) up off the ground with a specially shaped stick and when it was in the air, give it a second hard blow. He tipped the cat with his usual ease and in his own words,

... just as I was about to strike it a second time, a voice did suddenly dart from heaven into my soul, which said, 'Wilt thou leave thy sins, and go to heaven? Or have thy sins, and go to hell?' At this I was put to an exceeding maze; wherefore, leaving my cat upon the ground, I looked up to heaven, and was as if I had, with the eyes of my understanding, seen the Lord Jesus looking down upon me, as being very hotly displeased with me, and as if he did severely threaten me with some grievous punishment for these and other ungodly practices.

I have quoted this paragraph in full because, it must surely be one of the turning points of his life, one which he would never forget. He tells us, that there in the middle of the game, with his friends standing around him, he stood quite still, shocked into seeing his life as it really was and he knew then and there, that there was no longer any problem, no decision to make, his sins were so great that Jesus would *never* forgive him.

... miserable if I leave my sins, and but miserable if I follow them. I can but be damned; and if I must be so, I had as good be damned for many sins as be damned for few... The good Lord, whose mercy is unsearchable, forgive my transgressions!

He returned to the game.

CHAPTER ELEVEN

The Darkest Hour – Before The Dawn

However, as other Christians have found before and since, God does not let us decide such matters for ourselves. The darkest hour really does come before the dawn.

During the next few weeks or months, it is impossible to tell for how long, Bunyan appears to have given up all attempts at living a better life and wallowed in his bad behaviour. What his poor wife felt about all this or what sort of 'sins' he was committing, we do not know but the one which he seems to have been particularly proud of, and was indeed classed as a crime in the 1650s, was 'swearing'. That did not mean 'damning and blasting' but 'taking the name of God in vain', i.e. using the name of God or some other holy reference in a quite unsuitable and definitely unholy way. Using it not with respect but carelessly if not with scorn.

Accused of Swearing

Bunyan appears to have come from a home where such behaviour was normal. He records that he didn't know how to speak unless, 'I put an oath before and another behind, to make my words have authority...'

Then came what on the surface was the simplest of events and yet it was to prove one of the turning points in his life. One day when he was standing outside a neighbour's shop window and fooling about in his usual way, calling out to his friends and disturbing all the passers-by with his noisy and unsociable behaviour, the shopkeeper's wife called out to him to be quiet. She may just have felt that his rowdy behaviour was keeping people from entering her shop, or she may have been thoroughly disgusted with his rude manners but, whatever the reason, she gave him a good telling off.

Children maypole dancing at Elstow. Picture by kind permission of Mrs Worthington-Ellis. F9

She was no saint and had been known to utter oaths herself but she let him know that his continual swearing and cursing made her tremble and that she considered he was a thoroughly bad influence and likely to corrupt all the other young people of Elstow.

Once again one can see the state of conflict within him. Through the years he must have shrugged off or ignored innumerable reproaches and yet that one tirade from a woman whom he looked upon as a 'loose and ungodly wretch' brought him to a standstill. That this person, whom he had previously looked on with scorn, should see him as the '... ungodliest fellow for swearing', that she had ever heard, silenced him! He admits that he stood there with his head hanging and wished that he was a child again and had a strict father who would help him to grow up 'without this wicked way of swearing'.

He must have been at least 24 when this took place and a married man with a daughter; surely he thought it must be too late to change. He was condemned to go back home to his family, knowing that even the rougher element of the village despised him.

The young wife, whom he had chosen from the respectable God-fearing background, whatever did she think and what sort of father could he be to his poor little daughter, Mary? He never discloses in his books his attitude to Mary. She had been born blind and by this time he must have accepted that she would be blind for the rest of her life.

This time there was no 'voice from heaven', no vision of the Lord Jesus but, although each day after work he continued to meet his friends on the Green to play tip cat and other noisy games, he never again felt the need to swear. Apparently without difficulty or backsliding, the habit of a lifetime had ended.

Reading the Bible

The next stage of his conversion was when he met, 'one poor man who made profession of religion' who managed to interest him in the Bible. Bunyan wasn't ready yet for the teachings of Jesus or St Paul but thoroughly enjoyed the historical stories of the Old Testament. Coming across the Ten Commandments in their historical setting he was inspired to use them as a way to improve his daily life. Like most of us he had his successes and his failures but this time he found that when he slipped back it was not necessary for him to sink into a deep depression. He found that he could repent, tell God he was sorry, and ask for help that he might not repeat the fault; in that way he continued for about a year.

All these snippets of information are gleaned from his writing ten to 15 years later. They contain no reference to his home life, his wife or baby daughter because he is not writing about domesticity, only, as he remembers them, the stages whereby he changed from being a great sinner into a devout man.

Years later, if he did manage to arrange the occasional day's parole from prison, they were quite often spent visiting friends and acquaintances who were struggling with the problem of sin and the depression and helplessness which held them back from recovering their confidence in the forgiveness of God.

Respected by his Neighbours

His neighbours, who had known him for years and obviously regarded him as a thoroughly loud-mouthed, ill-behaved young man (and no doubt pitied his wife and wondered how she had ever come to marry him), were absolutely staggered by this change of behaviour. For the first few weeks, they probably commented in a critical way, thinking he must be ill or planning yet more mischief; then as the months went by they probably referred to his new pattern of behaviour as a nine day's wonder. Some of them even went up to him and commented on the change and he began to have a warm feeling inside to think that at last he was winning the respect of his neighbours. So much did he enjoy the feeling that others were now referring to him as an example of a godly man that he began to be quite proud of himself.

A Crisis of Conscience

In his attempts to live, what he saw, as a truly godly life, he gave up one of the things that he loved above all else, bell ringing. For this essentially emotional young man, this was one step too far and it pushed him to the very edge of sanity. When his conscience would no longer allow him to take part in the 'vain pleasure' of bell ringing he wasn't strong enough to stay away from the 'steeplehouse', and went along to watch. Then his demented conscience began to taunt him that to watch 'did not become religion neither'.

Torn by indecision, he forced himself to stay but then the thought came into his mind, 'How if one of the bells should fall?', so he moved and stood under one of the main beams, just in case! Even then his conscience wouldn't leave him alone; if the bells were swinging when they fell they would crush him to death even if he was standing under the beam. He moved back into the doorway where, although he couldn't watch his friends, he could listen to the bells.

The following week, as he stood in the doorway, the thought came into his head, 'How if the steeple itself should fall?'

For a few minutes he was strong enough to banish such a foolish thought but as he began to enjoy, vicariously, the movement on the ropes and the response of the bells, far up above him, he knew that if he stayed there any longer, the tower really would come down. He could see the falling masonry, feel the blows as the first stones hit him; chased by his imagination and demented conscience, he ran back home.

The 'Godly' Ladies of Bedford

From then on, it seems as though he became more introspective, more wildly depressed than before, until one day when he visited Bedford. There he overheard some ladies sitting out on their front doorsteps telling each other about the way that God had worked in their lives.

The poor young man who had made himself so distraught trying to solve his own problems, trying to make himself perfect in the eyes of God, heard these humble ladies describe the process whereby 'God' took on the making of perfection. 'God' objected to people who were so vain that they thought that they could improve their own lives, 'God' wanted men to turn to him for help and was anxious to help them help themselves.

The ladies must have realised that the young man was listening to them and no doubt they were shy at first to discuss such matters with a stranger but, when they realised how interested he was, they drew him into the conversation.

Over the years he had repeatedly tried to lift himself up from what he considered to be his sinful life and to start again, but repeatedly he had failed, the weight of his sins was too great. Now these ladies were saying that God both could and would give one a second chance and help one to resist Satan's temptations in the future. Previously, he had wished to become a child again and grow up in a godly home, now, these ladies talked of a 'new birth' something he had never even considered possible.

A Second Chance

Reluctantly, he left the ladies and went on his way to work but he returned to see them again and again. Unlike him, they were full of joy and how he envied their faith and happiness.

He thought of the so-called believers that he knew in the village who would go to church and under cover of worship would go to sleep or exchange gossip. He thought of men that he knew who were considered godly, but who would swear like troopers as soon as things went wrong and he returned once more to studying his Bible.

He struggled on desperately searching for a message and exhausting himself physically, mentally and emotionally. He read other books which only tended to add to his confusion. He studied the New

Testament and the letters of St Paul and returned yet again to the ladies in Bedford but their happiness was unattainable; it was not for him.

As happens in some Evangelical Churches today, where the Holy Spirit is present and many of the congregation receive great joy, other members of the congregation may appear to be shut out from the emotional excitement and say, 'Why them? Why not me?' and then, 'What have I done wrong? What am I doing wrong?' So once again Bunyan was near despair.

How could he tell if he had been chosen, been elected as one who should have a second chance? Worse still, supposing he was not one of those chosen, what then?

Before he had met with these ladies talking on their doorsteps he had not known that rebirth – a second chance – was possible. Now that he knew it was possible, what could he do to be chosen? He was obsessed. He read, he prayed, he questioned everybody that he met.

The time scale of this poor man's misery is difficult to assess. In his spiritual biography he suggests that it was almost a year before the ladies realised how distressed he was and introduced him to their minister, John Gifford, who, although he was not episcopally ordained and had served in the Royalist army, had been appointed to St John's Church Bedford in 1650.

John Gifford

Back in 1640, when Bunyan was only 12, the vicar of St Paul's Church Bedford had been in trouble because he allowed some of his congregation to receive communion without coming up to the altar rails. Three men who had defended him had become followers of this inspired 'lecturer', John Gifford, who had until the end of the war been a major in the Royalist army. So impressed were they by his preaching and teaching that when the Royalist vicar of St John's church lost the living in 1653, they were able to arrange with their colleagues on the council* that John Gifford should be appointed.

From *Grace Abounding*, it is impossible to tell how long Bunyan had struggled on his own, doing as so many people had done before and

*Bedford Borough Council were patrons of the living and under Cromwell, it was no longer necessary for an incumbent to be ordained by a bishop.

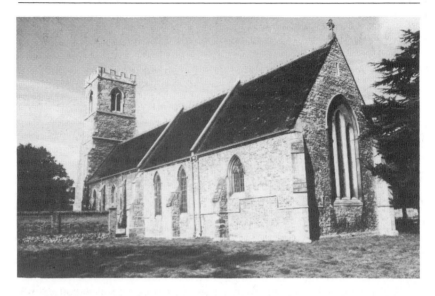

St John's Church, Bedford where John Gifford was the minister when Bunyan was baptised. F8

Renhold Church decorated for Christmas 1986. This would have been forbidden when the Puritans were in control. H7

since, desperately searching the Bible for help; one minute uplifted by joy, the next thrown into despair by an apparently contradictory story. One writer would appear to offer hope of salvation while another would cry 'too late'. Which one was right? Which one could he rely on?

Henri Talon* examining the stages of Bunyan's conversion and that of other similar tormented Christians, suggests that 'Bunyan could never have gained peace had he not entered a church capable of satisfying his need for human fellowship' and, undoubtedly, Gifford, who had struggled his own way through to belief, was from then on, a continual source of help and encouragement.

Yet the struggle was nowhere near ending. He had already noticed about men or women who had already been converted that, 'They shone, they walked like a people that carried the broad seal of heaven about them'.

Now more and more he wondered 'Why not me'. 'Is it too late?' 'Has God already "chosen" these people of Bedford who shall be saved?'

Gifford invited him to visit his home on occasions when he was holding discussion evenings, when he was helping other people and listening as to '... the dealings of God with their souls'.

To me, it seems as though at first this was a process which nearly drove him to despair. Listening to the struggles of others, maybe men who had never known the carnal and worldly temptations that he had faced. He had given up his bell-ringing and games on the village green but instead of finding inner peace and salvation he was haunted by nightmares and had completely lost his power of logical thought and concentration.

Day and night an inner voice taunted him and challenged him to 'Sell Jesus' to give up the struggle and to enjoy life as he had done back in Elstow during the early months of his marriage. At last, exhausted to the point of physical collapse, he let his will snap. For days or weeks, it is possible that even Bunyan himself did not know for how long, to use a modern expression, he 'went completely off the rails'. In his own words: 'And now was I both a burthen and a terror to myself'.

We will never know what his poor family were suffering throughout these months, nor of course, how wild his behaviour really became but it appears that despite everything he still read his Bible, because he was occasionally encouraged by a phrase such as:

*Henri Talon *John Bunyan*, the chapter on 'The Valley of the Shadow'.

... and the blood of Jesus Christ his Son
cleanseth us from all sin.*

For a few hours his depression lifted but soon it was back again and
as he compared himself with St Peter and others, who despite their
sins had held on with desperate determination to the love of Christ, he
felt that everything was combining to kill him.

It appears that his depression and the knowledge of his foolishly,
wild behaviour, kept him away from his friends at St John's Church.
Indeed, so great were his feelings of guilt that one day, in Bedford he
experienced an almost schizophrenic vision. He thought that he saw
the rays of the sun trying to avoid his head, the cobble stones trying to
avoid touching his feet and the nearby houses leaning backwards away
from him, because he had deserted his Saviour, the Lord, Jesus Christ.

Only an inner voice which reassured him, 'This sin is not unto
death', kept him from eventual insanity.

Within the next few days he begged God to show him a sign that he
was not forsaken and at once, the inner voice replied, 'I have loved thee
with an everlasting love'.

He went home and for the first time in months, went to bed happy
and woke up refreshed. There were more bouts of doubt and
depression to come but each one was shorter than the last.

At one point the inner voice broke into his thoughts, repeating over
and over again, 'My grace is sufficient for thee', and he clung
desperately to that message, until, at last, the struggle was over and
Bunyan came out of the clouds of depression to meet his Lord.

He was feeling anxious in case the cloud of depression should return
when he again heard the confident, comforting voice, 'Thy
righteousness is in Heaven' and with 'the eyes of my soul' he saw 'Jesus
Christ at God's right hand...'. There was his righteousness, on God's
right hand. Wherever he was, whatever he was doing, however badly
he behaved, God would never ask of him his righteousness; God
already had it, in the form of Jesus Christ himself.

'The same yesterday, today, and for ever'.

His terrors were over; his thoughts were now obsessed with the
knowledge and love of Jesus Christ.

Shortly afterwards, he joined the church at Bedford and was
baptised by John Gifford in the River Ouse.

*1st Letter of St John, Chapter 1, Verse 7.

CHAPTER TWELVE

John Bunyan becomes a Preacher

John Gifford himself had not found it easy to come to terms with the undoubted restrictions imposed on members of the Independent church. He had had some medical training either before or during the Civil War and when he came to Bedford he had taken up the position of physician left vacant by the resignation of the elderly Dr Banister.

As an ex-Royalist soldier, it appears that he found Parliamentary Bedford both quiet and dull. Like Bunyan he too lived a wild, ungodly life until a book that he had read led him to a religious crisis, after which he had actively sought out the members of the Independent church and had eventually become their leader.*

So he put no pressure on the young John Bunyan to join the church. However when one day he burst into the rectory, radiating the joy of his new-found love of Christ, the committee were delighted to accept him as a member and witness his baptism at nearby, Duck Mill, Bedford.

Not all those who attended an Independent church became members; there was a careful selection process and the behaviour of even long-standing members was watched, as was that of their family and close friends.

John Bunyan begins to Preach

As always, timescales are difficult to calculate; Bunyan suggests that several years went by before some of the senior members, '... The most able for judgement and holiness of life ... did perceive that God

*For details of this early group of 'Independent' Christians and of John Gifford's experience in the Royalist army before coming to Bedford, see John Brown – Chapter 5.

St John's Rectory, Bedford where John Bunyan visited John Gifford. Possibly 'The Interpreter's House' from The Pilgrim's Progress. F8

The pool where John Bunyan was baptised. (Flooded January 1988). F8

had counted me worthy to understand something of his will in his holy
and blessed word, . . .' They then invited him to address their meetings
occasionally.

At first he was reluctant but on two separate occasions they
persuaded him and he was so encouraged by their kind words and
helpful comments that he tells us, 'After this, sometimes when some of
them did go into the country to teach, they would also that I should go
with them'. He was still too timid to address these village meetings and
was surprised to find how grateful some members of the audience were
to receive his help and guidance afterwards.

The Death of John Gifford

Bunyan's timescale would lead us to believe that he did not become a
regular preacher for some years after his baptism around 1653.
However, the death of the much loved minister John Gifford, early in
September 1655 and the events which followed may have obliged him
to start somewhat earlier than his writings suggest.

The new leader was a young man called John Burton; he had poor
health and was sometimes too ill to travel out to the villages, so in fact it
may have been as an unknown writer added to the church record
book,★ 'Mr Bunyan began to preach some time in the year 1656'.

Whenever he started he very soon found that he had a gift both to
hold an audience and to reach out a reassuring hand to support men
and women who felt separated from the love of God by the weight of
their sins.

Bunyan and the Quakers

The next stage in Bunyan's ministry came very quickly.

During 1654, the Quaker, William Dewsbury, had visited
Bedfordshire and influenced several families who became the nuclei of
scattered groups who believed in his message of personal salvation. At
this stage in his religious life, Bunyan felt strongly that they were
seriously confused, if not downright heretical in their beliefs. On
several occasions he disputed with them publicly and was most

★The Church Book of the Bunyan Meeting.

concerned that the converts that he was helping to strengthen would become confused, or even abandon their search for faith.

Vera Brittain*, writing in the complete religious freedom of the 1940s noted,

> There was no essential difference between John Bunyan and George Fox; Fox's belief in an inner light merely carried to its logical conclusion the Puritan witness against formal religion in the name of which John went to prison. Both alike taught the poor and humble to use their minds and apply their imagination in the service of God.

The First Pamphlet

However, in 1656 he was so concerned about the damage that he felt the Quakers were doing, that this 28-year-old craftsman, who had only the minimum of formal education, wrote and published a pamphlet, *Some Gospel Truths Opened, by that unworthy servant of Christ, John Bunyan of Bedford, by the Grace of God, preacher of the Gospel of his dear Son.*

John Burton wrote a preface and it is interesting that among other compliments that he paid Bunyan, he wrote, 'He hath through grace taken . . . experiences of the temptations of Satan, which do more fit a man for that mighty work of preaching the Gospel than all university learning and degrees that can be had'.

This pamphlet was refuted by Edward Burrough, a young Quaker who published *The True Faith of the Gospel of Peace, contended for in the spirit of meekness . . . against the secret opposition of John Bunyan, a professed minister in Bedfordshire.*

Bunyan replied with *A Vindication of Gospel Truths Opened.* This ended the published debate but Bunyan must have realised that pamphlets could reach a wider audience than preaching. In 1658 and 1659, he published two more ambitious booklets on Biblical themes, *A Few Sighs From Hell* and *The Doctrine of the Law and of Grace.*

In The Steps of John Bunyan - - p.160. When some years later, Bunyan shared a prison cell with some Quakers and had both time and maturity he found that they did indeed have beliefs in common.

The Death of Oliver Cromwell

Even while Bunyan was writing the former booklet Oliver Cromwell lay critically ill. As has been noted, he was a determined supporter of the Independent churches and while he was in control of the country they could meet quite openly. Whether Bunyan and others like him were already discussing the changes they might expect to meet in the years to come we do not know but in his foreword to this third booklet, which was published only days before the death of Cromwell, he includes a prayer that the Lord would help him when necessary to turn the other cheek and to show patience when up against the rages of the world.

The Personal Touch

Although this is one of his more serious works of religious thought, it nevertheless includes some illustrations from his own life. The smith's dog which once settled by the foot of the anvil fails to move even though the sparks fly up into its face. The man who when young preferred reading ballads, chap-books and fables rather than the Bible.

He also makes reference to men who despise those who are not 'gentlemen', and who do not speak Hebrew, Greek and Latin.

Bunyan and Cambridge University

So popular was his style of preaching that Bunyan received invitations from an ever-widening area and before long, this included crossing the borders of Cambridgeshire. On some of these visits, there were members of the university in the audience.

One or two of them were so shocked that 'the tinker', as they nicknamed him, should set himself up as a preacher, that they heckled during his talks, remained to argue with him afterwards and published letters of complaint. They challenged his right to instruct others when he could not read the original scriptures for himself. They meant, of course, that he was unable to read Greek and Hebrew. He replied that they were unable to read the 'original' documents themselves, due to them not being available. The scholars at once replied that they had available to them true copies. 'And I,' Bunyan is reported as replying 'believe the English Bible to be a true copy also'!

This and many similar arguments were brought against him by different scholars but other Cambridge men, such as Henry Denne stood up for him. In a pamphlet published in 1659 he wrote in support of the 'tinker' who strove to 'mend souls as well as kettles and pans'.

William Dell, master of Gonville and Caius College, was also rector of Yelden in the very north of Bedfordshire. On Christmas Day 1659, he invited Bunyan to take the services and preach in his church. Some of his parishioners objected but during the period known as 'The Commonwealth' this was still legal and there was nothing they could do to prevent it*.

Independent Preachers at Risk

As the political situation became increasingly unstable so the Independent churches realised that they might soon be in danger. Bunyan had already had a warning; back in March 1658, six months before the death of Cromwell, he had been arrested by the constable of Eaton Socon and charged to appear at the next meeting of the Assize Court. There is no record that the case actually came to court and the incident may have been a warning by the local vicar that he would not have itinerant preachers in his parish.

As the army and politicians struggled to control the country the Independent churches had more such 'warnings' and the Quakers were openly persecuted.

The Restoration of the Monarchy

By 1660 the majority of the country's leaders were resigned to the fact that politically it was necessary to invite the son of King Charles I to become King Charles II of England. Even the landowners of Parliamentary Bedfordshire had to agree that it was necessary. The Royalist landowners were, of course, delighted and Lord Bruce of Ampthill went over to The Hague to issue the invitation to Prince Charles. The Earl of Cleveland and his son Lord Wentworth, of Toddington, who were in exile with their chosen king, rode into

---

*The following June they complained about this and other matters to the House of Lords.

Oak Cottage, Ravensden. Typical of the cottages Bunyan would have passed on his way to Yelden. G6

London with him on 29 May 1660 and helped to organise the official celebrations. The family of Sir John Osborne had managed to 'buy back' the sequestered, Chicksands estate and the newly crowned king made him a baronet. Sir Lewis Dyve, who had spent some years imprisoned in the Tower of London, had escaped to the Continent, where he continued fighting on behalf of the Crown; he died in obscurity. It was due to the sequestration of his property that the Manor of Sewell (near Houghton Regis) passed to Henry Brandreth.

On the other hand, John Okey of Brogborough Park (near Ampthill) and others who had actually signed the death warrant of Charles I, quickly left the country.*

Inner Peace

In his spiritual life Bunyan was at last enjoying a period of inner peace and the happiness that came from knowing that the Lord was daily with him in his work. He appears all this time to have been supporting his family by working as a tinker, making simple repairs to household and farm implements, as he travelled the roads of three or four

---

*Okey was arrested two years later, brought home, tried and executed.

counties on formal or informal preaching trips. He had overcome his initial diffidence at speaking in public and had learned to handle an audience; which hecklers to ignore and which to use in putting over his message. He would always have a special sympathy with people who felt that they were separated from the love of God by the enormity of their sins.

> Thus I went on for the space of two years, crying out against men's sins, and their fearful state because of them. After which the Lord came in upon my soul with some sure peace and comfort through Christ; for he did give me many sweet discoveries of his blessed grace through him.

With this deeper understanding he was able to widen the subject of his talks and of his writing.

CHAPTER THIRTEEN

John Bunyan is Arrested

It is generally thought that John and Mary moved into St Cuthbert Street in 1655. If so, their blind daughter, Mary, would have been five years old, and their second daughter, Elizabeth, who had also been christened at Elstow, was nearly two.

During the next few years two more children were born; John, soon after their arrival in Bedford and Thomas, two or three years later. Parish registers were not always kept up during this period and if the boys were baptised, the records have not survived.

The Fears of the Magistrates

Although Charles had promised liberty to those that he described as having 'tender consciences' and that no man should be arrested for 'differences of opinion in matters of religion, that do not disturb the peace of the Kingdom', reluctantly and for various reasons, landowners, and those expected to keep the peace, began to realise that they would have to control or even prevent the gatherings of Independent church members. It would be too easy for political agitators to use these meetings to cause trouble.

Other Justices were against these preachers because they thought that a man who encouraged independent thought would also encourage independent action. Also, they were afraid that an uneducated preacher who was doing the job of an ordained clergyman would make other uneducated men think they had the right to replace magistrates and other officials.

The 'Laudian' Clergy Return

Even before legislation was passed to support them, the sequestered clergy were demanding that they be returned to their livings and within a few months an Act was passed which supported them.

William Dell resigned straight away from his appointment at Cambridge University and two years later lost the Rectory at Yelden. Thorne returned to St Mary's Bedford and, at St John's, where the much loved 'Bros. Burton' had recently died, Theodore Crowley was again presented to the living.

The Death of Mary

During this period when church ceremonies were not being recorded, the wife who had stood by Bunyan through all his years of depression and who had kept the home together and supported him, died and was presumably buried at St Cuthbert's Church. Left alone with four small children, the eldest being blind, he quickly remarried. We know very little about his new wife at this time except that she was very young, called 'Elizabeth', that she took full responsibility for his young family and that she was soon pregnant herself.

The Enforcement of Prayer Book Service

When the Bedford magistrates published an order for 'the publick reading of the Liturgy of the Church of England', Bunyan, his committee and presumably his new wife, must have known that he was at risk of arrest. There was no law or bye-law which forbade outdoor meetings but whereas the magistrates appear to have waived the arrest at Eaton Socon, now they would take seriously any local arrest.

An Invitation to Preach

When an invitation arrived for Bunyan to address a public meeting on a farm at Lower Samsell, a hamlet near Harlington, he knew that he had to make a desperately difficult decision.

The farmer was a friend of his and he particularly did not want to disappoint him and his friends, so he set out for Harlington. However, when he arrived, he found his friend waiting for him and before he even got into the house he was warned that the local landlord and Justice of the Peace, Francis Wingate, had issued a warrant for his arrest should he even attempt to start preaching.

In 1765, a manuscript was at last published *A Relation of the Imprisonment of Mr John Bunyan* in which Bunyan set out quite clearly the events of 12 November 1660, and excerpts from the days, that followed (see p. 129 in Chapter 14). He tells us that his host was most nervous for him, suggested that they cancel the meeting and that Bunyan should return straight home. He had replied, 'No, by no means. I will not stir; neither will I have the meeting dismissed for this. Come, be of good cheer! Let us not be daunted; our cause is good; we need not be ashamed of it. To preach God's Word is so good a work, that we shall be well rewarded if we suffer for that.'

Then he went outside on his own and walking around the paddock, thought of his newly-converted friends and their discouragement if it was known that he had walked away from danger. He went back indoors and as soon as they were ready, opened the Bible, and suggested that they should start by asking God to bless their meeting.

The Arrest

However, before he had finished the first prayer, the village constable had arrived and forced him to leave the room. It appears that he managed to get back for a few minutes or else the group surrounded him outside, because he records that before he left he was able to offer them a few words of counsel and encouragement.

The constable was edgy and worried by the responsibility and hurried him away but when they got back to Harlington, Wingate was away from home. One of Bunyan's friends offered a surety that if the constable allowed him to take Bunyan to his home for the night, he would guarantee to bring him back in the morning, this was agreed.

Francis Wingate JP

Francis Wingate, a local magistrate of the same age but from a very different background to John Bunyan, was very much aware of the political unrest in London and elsewhere. Knowing that the people of Bedfordshire had previously been firm supporters of Parliament, he was worried that plotters might use Bunyan's meetings to stir up trouble.

He questioned the constable to discover if anyone was carrying anything in the way of an offensive weapon and was apparently surprised when he reported that they were just a few people who had met together to 'preach and hear the word'.

The account of the interview, as written down by Bunyan some years later, suggests that Wingate then asked him a few impromptu questions, such as why he didn't concentrate on his own work and leave off doing the work of an ordained preacher, which for him was now illegal. Bunyan pointed out that as a tinker he could quite well carry out his trade in conjunction with his travels to instruct and counsel people. This answer annoyed Wingate who threatened to stop all such meetings. Bunyan kept calm and when Wingate threatened him with prison he was allowed to call in his friends who were prepared to stand surety for his good behaviour. Wingate then explained to these friends that it would be their responsibility to stop him from preaching and that if they did not they would lose their money.

At once Bunyan pointed out that this was pointless because where-ever he went he would 'counsel, comfort, exhort and teach the people' that he should meet and wouldn't cease to preach the word of God. Further, he considered this more worthy of commendation than of blame. After that statement, it was pointless to discuss bail and so Wingate left the room to prepare the papers which would commit Bunyan to prison to await the next Quarter Sessions.

Meanwhile, Wingate's father-in-law, Dr Lindall, came into the room. He may have been the cause of the arrest because he was vicar of Harlington and it appears that Bunyan was already aware of his animosity towards unordained preachers. Lindall taunted Bunyan for meddling with things which were beyond his understanding but refused to debate with him.

Wingate came back into the room, gave the constable the papers and within minutes they were outside and ready to set off for Bedford prison. However, two others from the meeting persuaded the constable to wait while they went in to talk to Wingate. Eventually a message came for them to return to the house. If Bunyan would repeat a certain, carefully worded phrase, he would be free.

Stevington Baptist Church, founded by a group of Christians connected with John Bunyan. D6

William Foster

Bunyan was dubious but agreed to return; as they approached the study, via a dark passageway, yet another man appeared, Wingate's brother-in-law, William Foster JP (later Dr Foster). Having pretended ignorance of the whole episode and demanded to know what Bunyan was doing in the house, he then advised him to give the requested promise. He knew, he said, that his brother was '. . . very loth to send him to prison'.

Bunyan tried to explain his purpose in gathering a crowd of people together but Foster did not want discussion; he made one final statement, '. . . if you will say you will call the people no more together you may have your liberty; if not, you must be sent away to prison'.

It was obvious that neither would change or modify their point of view. Foster went into Wingate's room and told him that he should send not only Bunyan but also all his associates to prison.

So Bunyan, accompanied by the constable, rode off to Bedford prison with 'God's comfort in his soul'.

CHAPTER FOURTEEN

Imprisoned in Bedford Gaol

In 20th century England it is hard for us to understand how Bunyan could leave his new wife and much loved children to spend so many years in prison, even though it was only five minutes away from his home and his family could occasionally visit him. It is doubtful, when he first entered in November 1660, if he had any idea that he was starting such a long prison sentence.

Informal meetings such as that held at Harlington were not yet illegal and Bunyan was actually arrested under an Act which had been passed in the reign of Queen Elizabeth.

> If any person above sixteen years of age, shall forbear coming to church for one month, or persuade any other person to abstain from hearing divine service, or receiving the communion accordingly to law, or come to any unlawful assembly, conventicle or meeting – every such person shall be imprisoned, without bail, until he conform....

It went on to state that for repeated offences they must stay in gaol until the next Assize Court. Repeated offences could bring a judgement of transportation to 'foreign plantations'.

Regardless of the punishment, Bunyan was most reluctant to give in to pressure from the magistrates or from some of his own advisors. He was so concerned as to how his actions would influence the weaker members of the various groups that he had recently visited.

From his personal point of view he was almost happy; convinced that he was carrying out the will of God. Even when Mr Crompton, the Elstow magistrate, first promised to sign bail papers and then changed his mind and refused, Bunyan remained cheerful and content. He had spent much time meditating on the advantages and disadvantages of freedom and had come to the conclusion that God could make more use of him in prison than outside.

Medieval cross in Knotting church yard. E3

The Will of God

In his spiritual autobiography he records: 'I did meet my God sweetly in the prison again, comforting of me, and satisfying of me that it was His will and mind that I should be there.'

He also records that he was not anxious for his future safety:

> . . . I lie waiting the good will of God, to do with me as he pleaseth; knowing that not one hair of my head can fall to the ground without the will of my Father which is in heaven. Let the rage and malice of men be ever so great, they can do no more, nor go any farther, than God permits them: but when they have done their worst, 'we know that all things work together for good to them that love God' Romans VIII 28. Farewell.

The last phrase comes from the King James translation of St Paul's letter to the Romans and continues:

> to them who are the called according to his purpose.

The translators of The New English Bible, (1961) have a slightly different emphasis:

> and in everything, as we know, he co-operates for good with those who love God, and are called according to his purpose.

Reading the verses of this chapter we can see how, through the centuries, words have slightly changed their meaning. Verse 35 in the King James' translation:

> Who shall separate us from the love of Christ? Shall tribulation, or distress or persecution or famine ... ?

Has a different emphasis today from the New English Bible translation:

> Then what can separate us from the love of Christ? Can affliction, or hardship? Can persecution, hunger ... ?

Maybe this is why we find some of Bunyan's writing hard to understand.

The Assize Court

So for the next six or seven weeks, Bunyan stayed in prison waiting for the Quarter Sessions, which were held in an old building known as the 'Chapel of Herne'. The judges were five local landowners who in varying degrees had all been Royalist sympathisers.

Sir John Kelynge of Southill was the chairman; because of his loyalty to King Charles I he had spent some years in prison and had had to wait nearly thirty years for preferment at the bar. He was not likely to be sympathetic towards John Bunyan.

The charge included the indictment that he had, 'devilishly and perniciously' abstained from attending church and that he was a 'common upholder of several unlawful meetings and conventicles to the great disturbance and distraction of the good subjects of this kingdom...'.

The clerk asked Bunyan how he reacted to the charge and when he replied that he was a 'common frequenter of the church of God', he and Kelynge were instantly disagreeing as to what they meant by such words as, 'church' i.e. a building or a congregation of Christians.

The Meaning of Biblical Phrases

Kelynge challenged him as to his authority to preach and Bunyan quoted from the first letter that St Peter wrote to the scattered groups of Christians of his day:

> As every man hath received the gift, even so minister the same one to another, as good stewards of the manifold grace of God. If any man speak, let him speak as the oracles of God; if any man minister, let him do it as of the ability which God giveth:... (Peter 1, Chapter 4, v. 10 and 11).

Had Bunyan had the New English translation to call upon, his case would have been even stronger. Peter instructs his readers to share whatever gifts they have been given and specifically asks members of the group: 'Are you a speaker? Speak as if you uttered oracles of God'.

Kelynge said that St Peter meant men to speak out within their own families. Bunyan replied that if it was good within the family it must be even better to preach to groups outside. If that was what Kelynge considered to be a sin then he would continue sinning.

Kelynge pounced, 'Then you confess the indictment, do you not?' he asked.

Bunyan saw how he had been led and admitted that he and his friends had met to help and encourage each other and had been aware of the 'sweet comforting presence of the Lord' helping them. If that was a fault, he must admit to being guilty.

Kelynge was content; in a few minutes, with the minimum of fuss or argument, he had won.

The Sentence

Bunyan was sent back to the county gaol on the corner of Silver Street and High Street. He was warned that if he did not agree to attend his parish church when he was next called before the justices in three months time, and/or refused to 'leave his preaching', he would be 'banished the realm'.

So Bunyan returned to the cells and records that, far from being depressed by the hearing, his heart was 'sweetly refreshed', that Jesus had been with him in the court and had truly helped him to find the right words to use when responding to the judge.

The Second Quarter Sessions

When the date was approaching for the next meeting of the justices, Bunyan began to wonder what form the next hearing would take. The authorities were possibly more worried than he was; the Act under which he was being held was still that of Queen Elizabeth but Kelynge had been quite right when he warned Bunyan that a re-appearance in court could mean transportation.

The Royalist landowners and the expelled, Laudian clergymen were now settling back into their estates and there was a general feeling that everyone must work to create a united and settled community. Few, if any, of the Bedfordshire landowners would want to see one of their neighbours sent out to work on the plantations.

The Justices' Clerk

The Justices sent Cobb, their clerk, to see Bunyan to try and persuade him to conform. The clerk started in a friendly way, addressing Bunyan as 'neighbour' and giving him a friendly warning. The Justices had sent him with a warning that they had every intention of prosecuting if he didn't promise to conform to the Church of England. Bunyan then pointed out that the law by which he was imprisoned was not intended to stop men like himself from preaching to comparatively small groups of local people. Cobb was well aware of this but pointed out that all speakers, even political agitators, would claim the same thing even if, like some political agitators, they really intended to cause a riot.

> Yet it doth not follow (said Bunyan) that because they did so, therefore all others will do so. I look upon it as my duty to behave myself, under the King's government, both as becomes a man and a Christian; and if an occasion were offered me, I should willingly manifest my loyalty to my prince, both by word and deed.

This passage comes from Bunyan's own account of his imprisonment and I quote it in full because it is Bunyan's own declaration*. However, these sympathies did not suit Cobb who had to return to the Justices without a promise of reform. He tried another approach –

... you may have your liberty to exhort your neighbour in private discourse, so be you do not call together an assembly of people; and truly you may do much good to the Church of Christ, if you would go this way; and this you may do, and the law not abridge you of it. It is your private meetings** that the law is against.

As quick as a flash, Bunyan asked why he could do good to one person but not to two, if to two, why not four, to eight and so on. If the authorities considered that he could do good to an individual who came to listen to him in the privacy of his own home – how could they step in to stop him doing good to more than one person in a public place?

Cobb's approach became slightly more irritable, especially when Bunyan said that he refused to believe that Queen Elizabeth had intended the oppressing of any of God's ordinances.

Again and again Cobb returned to the same theme and tried to persuade Bunyan to wait and see what legal changes came in the future – or – to let his case (that he should be allowed to preach in public) be judged by two impartial people.

At once Bunyan asked how anyone could tell if their judgement was more reliable than his? Then Cobb put into words what many frustrated people have thought throughout the centuries, when arguing with someone of a different belief, 'who shall be judge between you? For you take the Scriptures one way, and they another'.

They argued on and on concerning the judgement of the church, the government and those in authority. Bunyan insisting that he was more than prepared to obey the laws set by men provided only they did not clash with the laws of God as expressed in Scripture. Eventually, Cobb realised that he was wasting his time and he drew the meeting to a close, begging Bunyan to think over all the points that they had discussed, before the Quarter Sessions met in a few days time. He concluded by saying, 'You may do much good if you continue still in the land; but, alas! What benefit will it be to your friends, or what good can you do to them, if you should be sent away beyond the seas ...'.

*A Relation of the Imprisonment of Mr John Bunyan.
**He meant what we would call, 'public' meetings.

A Long Stay in Prison

It would be easy to see John Bunyan as a withdrawn ascetic, a frustrated, would-be scholar, only too pleased to withdraw from the world to study, read and write. However, from passages that he included in his own account of his time in prison, we can tell this was not at all the case.

In the early days, the prison was not too crowded, the discipline not too strict, and it was possible to have food sent in from outside. From time to time his family and friends could visit him and he knew that they would try and help support Elizabeth and the children but he must have been desperately worried.

John Bunyan's Wife, Elizabeth

The immediate effect of Bunyan's imprisonment was that his wife, Elizabeth, went into premature labour. For over a week it was touch and go; her life was saved but she lost the baby and remained weak for some time. When she was strong again she often visited the prison and took a full part in the discussions as to how his friends and family could best help her husband.

The Death of John Burton

The position was made more difficult because John Burton, the minister at St John's church had recently died and the Independents on Bedford council were no longer strong enough to appoint another un-ordained minister.

The Loss of St John's Church

The ageing Theodore Crowley returned to live in St John's vicarage and take services at the church, and the Independent congregation met in each others' houses, farms, barns or wherever they could. As the years passed and their meetings were banned, these places were frequently changed and the services often took place late at night.

A Relation of the Imprisonment of Mr John Bunyan

The written account that he kept of his time in prison was a manuscript, which at that time it was not safe for him to publish. It passed through the Bunyan family as an heirloom until it was finally sold by his great-granddaughter, Hannah, in 1765, for five guineas. It was then published under the above title.

In this he tells us that, when he realised that he might end up in prison, he had worried about two things. Firstly, he might eventually lose his life and secondly, even if he survived, he could end up by never seeing his wife and children again.

Shut up in prison for weeks on end, these problems went round and round in his mind.

Family Fears

There were many passages in the Bible which could comfort a man who was facing death and others such as Jeremiah 49 v. 11 'Leave thy fatherless children, I will preserve them alive, and let thy widows trust in me' which assured him that God would care for his loved ones. Nevertheless he agonised about these things. Execution might give him the chance to make an important declaration of the love of God but, equally, he might also give way to fear and damage the reputation of his church.

Transportation did not only mean that he would be sent across the sea to work in the plantations but also meant that all his property would be sold to pay his fare. He felt that he was 'a man who was pulling down his house upon the head of his wife and children' and yet he knew he was right and wrote over and over again – 'I must do it'.

Although he continued to spend hours in prayer and Bible study, he could not escape from the terrible loneliness and distress caused by the separation from his family. The more he missed their company the more he worried about them, especially poor blind Mary. Despite all the problems of the last few years he had been able to provide her with a safe and happy home. Now the sacrifice he was making by staying in prison, risking transportation and even loss of life was as nothing to the risk he was taking on behalf of his poor blind daughter.

CHAPTER FIFTEEN

Elizabeth Bunyan Fights for a Pardon

The Quarter Sessions were postponed because it was announced that King Charles II would be crowned on 23 April. As was customary 'divers prisoners' would be released and many people hoped that Bunyan would be one of them.

However, when the list was made up, Bunyan's name was not included. Because he had refused to plead 'guilty' or 'not guilty', Kelynge had entered his silence as a confession of guilt. Not only was he left off the list for pardon but he would not appear before the magistrates when the next Quarter Sessions were held, or before the Assize Judges when they visited Bedford.

The Convicted Prisoner

Bunyan was now classed as a convicted prisoner and his only hope was to appeal for a pardon during the twelve months of clemency following the coronation.

One improvement was that he knew now that he had twelve months before a punishment worse than prison could be enforced.

There were endless discussions as to how he should go about the formal process of asking for a pardon. The friends outside the prison had heard that a certain Lord Barkwood might be able to help them and it was decided that Elizabeth should go to London and ask him for advice.

How she managed this we do not know; whether she travelled the long weary journey on a carrier's cart or whether one of the friends took her on the back of his horse. Having arrived in an unfamiliar city it must have been an almost impossible task both to find and then to approach Lord Barkwood. It is possible that friends in London arranged both the journey and the meeting.

Elizabeth Bunyan meets Lord Barkwood

Lord Barkwood listened sympathetically to Elizabeth's story. The law case was obviously complicated and any judgement made by John, now Sir John Kelynge would be difficult to set aside; he was a rising man. Barkwood told Elizabeth that he would have to discuss the case with other members of the House of Lords. When she returned to see him he said that they were agreed that the only way for her husband to get a pardon would be by appealing to the Assize Judges on circuit when they next visited Bedford.

The Assize Judges visit Bedford

If Elizabeth visited London soon after the coronation, it would probably have been in May or June 1661. The Assize Judges were not due to visit Bedford until August, so the Bunyans had a few weeks in which to make their plans. They were sure that the local magistrates would prevent his appearance in court and set out to find some other way of approaching the judges. Bunyan tells us that he 'would not leave any possible means unattempted that might be lawful'. So he carefully wrote out a petition, asking that he might be considered for a Royal Pardon. When he was satisfied with it he copied it out three times and discussed with Elizabeth the best way they could get these copies to the judges.

Elizabeth Bunyan presents her Petitions

There were a great many formalities when the judges visited a county town. They not only judged the more serious cases which were waiting for them but also had various semi-private and public meetings. They would meet local councillors, magistrates and landowners concerning administrative and legal problems that had cropped up locally or nationally. For some of their official business they wore both their wigs and official robes and each day there were one or more processions as they drove from one part of the town to another. Both of the expected judges were ex-Royalists and not likely to be very sympathetic, but Matthew Hale had been brought up by a guardian who was a Puritan and had some sympathy for men who wished for freedom to worship God in their own way. Because of this they probably planned in advance for her to give him the first petition and luckily she was able to get up to him and hand it over herself. He quickly glanced at it and said that he would see if there was anything that he could do to help them but that he doubted if it would be possible.

She wasn't so lucky with the other judge, Sir Thomas Twisden. She could not find an opportunity of getting up to him to hand over the petition, so in desperation she threw a copy into his coach! He stopped and looked at it but angrily told her to go away as there was no way they could examine the case of someone who had already been convicted. If her husband wanted to leave prison he must promise not to continue preaching. So that copy had been wasted and she decided to try and approach Judge Hale again, in case he had forgotten all about them.

She was lucky and managed to get into the court chamber. Apparently he recognised her and allowed her to come up to his table but, before she could hand over the petition, the local magistrate on duty, Sir Henry Chester from Lidlington, stepped up in front of her. He reminded Hale that Bunyan was already convicted and stated that he was a 'hot spirited fellow'.

Hale had no intention of offending the local bench and would not let her approach further.

The sheriff, who appears to have been sympathetic to Bunyan, suggested to Elizabeth that she should have one last attempt at approaching Hale while he was attending a meeting at The Swan.

Elizabeth Bunyan's Last Appeal

So the next day she bravely pushed her way into the upper room where the local magistrates and landowners were talking to the two judges. Standing amongst them she must have been trembling with fright. When there was a break in the discussion the sheriff or one of his aides must have given her a sign and she managed to speak loudly enough for both Hale and many other people to hear.

'My Lord,' she said, 'I make bold to come again to your lordship, to know what may be done with my husband.'

Hale sighed and repeated once more that there was nothing he could do to help a convicted prisoner.

'My Lord,' she replied, 'he is kept unlawfully in prison; they

The Swan, Bedford

clapped him up before there were any proclamations against the meetings'.

She went on to explain that he was not convicted; he had never been judged guilty or not guilty.

Before Hale could reply, one of the local magistrates that she did not recognise cut in, 'My Lord, he was lawfully convicted'.

Elizabeth felt herself getting even more upset and quickly tried to explain. When the justices had asked her husband to confess he had merely replied that he had attended several meetings where people had met to pray and listen to a preacher. Also, that these meetings had been blessed with the presence of God.

Judge Twisden then cut in and asked her what she thought they could do to help a 'breaker of the peace' once he had been found guilty.

Judge Hale sent for the statute book and while they waited she tried to explain once more that he was not lawfully convicted.

Justice Chester interfered again, 'My Lord, he was lawfully convicted.'

'It is false,' cried poor Elizabeth.

'But it is recorded, woman, it is recorded,' said Chester.

With dignity, Elizabeth refused to be drawn into an argument and turned directly towards Judge Hale. She explained to him how she had been to London and consulted Lord Barkwood. That she had handed him a petition and that he had discussed it with other members of the House of Lords. Then, making sure that both judges were listening, she explained how their advice had been to appeal to the assize judges (themselves) who would be able to help her, 'This he told me; and now I am come to you to see if anything may be done in this business, and you give neither releasement nor relief.'

The two judges made no reply and apparently busied themselves with other papers, while Chester, taking the opportunity provided by their silence, repeated yet again, 'He is convicted – it is recorded.'

'If it be, it is false,' cried poor Elizabeth.

'My Lord,' said Chester,* 'he is a pestilent fellow; there is not such a fellow in the country again.'

Judge Hale was getting impatient with such a pointless argument which was going round and round. He asked Elizabeth point blank if her husband was prepared to give up preaching.

'My Lord,' she said, 'he dares not leave preaching as long as he can speak.'

Hale gave up; he couldn't waste anymore time on such a fellow. Bunyan must do what he thought best; after all he was a troublemaker; they had wasted too much time on him already.

Poor, helpless Elizabeth, she must at times have agreed with Hale, only she was far too loyal to say so. Desperately she realised that Chester had caused Hale to get an entirely wrong picture of her beloved husband. She must make one more try before she returned to the prison where John would be waiting and would expect her to remember every word.

Stumbling, she tried to explain that her husband wasn't a

---

*Chester was related to the Vicar of Hitchin, one of the clergymen who bitterly resented the Independent preachers visiting their parishes and thus encouraging their parishioners not to attend the parish church.

troublemaker. All he wanted was to be free to travel around the countryside, plying his trade as a tinker and supporting his wife and children.

'My Lord, I have four small children, that cannot help themselves, one of which is blind, and we have nothing to live upon but the charity of good people.'

Hale looked at her in amazement. He couldn't believe such a young woman could possibly have four children. Elizabeth explained that she was their step-mother and that she had married Bunyan less than two years before. She told him about the loss of her own baby and how ill she had been.

This upset Hale who in some respects was a kindly man but once again Twisden interrupted and said that she was using her poverty as a way of gaining their sympathy. From what he had heard, Bunyan had earned more money as a preacher than he had by following his own calling.

Although Elizabeth did not get any help, it is amazing to think that Judge Hale was prepared to delay this important meeting, and keep the room full of landowners waiting, while he talked to a penniless woman. He was still interested in the case and asked, 'What is his calling?'

'A tinker, my Lord,' called out someone in the crowd.

'Yes,' said Elizabeth bitterly, 'and because he is a tinker and a poor man, therefore he is despised and cannot have justice.'

Hale wouldn't allow this; Elizabeth must be made to understand that it was her husband's situation, not his poverty which made it impossible for him to help her. Slowly he explained that because the local justices had interpreted her husband's words as a confession of guilt, he was not the person who could help her. Only the King could grant pardon to a convicted prisoner.

The only other advice he could give her was that she should ask for a 'Writ of Error'.*

Elizabeth did not really understand this (nor apparently did John Bunyan) but Chester did and he was very offended. He at once distracted Elizabeth by again telling Hale how much harm Bunyan would do if released and Twisden joined in, getting more and more heated and demanding that Hale should send her away.

---

*As today it was possible to ask for a re-trial if it could be proved that the original trial had been wrongly conducted.

Reluctantly the judge gave his final decision; she must try to get a pardon from the King or, what would probably be easier and cheaper, apply for the 'Writ of Error' which would wipe out the first trial.

She may never have heard this because Twisden was so angry that he had come down into the hall and while Chester was banging his own head in anger, Twisden looked as if he might strike Elizabeth!

She had utterly failed. If only they had allowed John to come and speak for himself; she was sure she had forgotten half the points he had told her to make. With tears streaming down her face, she left the hall, and went to find her husband.

Bunyan returns to Preaching

It is more than likely that Bunyan was half expecting her to fail. He must have known that Twisden and most of the local magistrates would have been against his release. Nevertheless it was disappointing, because it made Elizabeth's journey to London seem a complete waste of time and money. Maybe this is what encouraged him to undertake what proved to be a rather foolish journey.

The judges were not due to return to Bedford until 19 January 1662, nine months after the coronation.

The sheriff and officials in charge of the prison were satisfied that Bunyan did not intend to cause trouble and turned a blind eye when the gaoler let Bunyan visit his own home. Once the gaoler found that he could trust Bunyan to return to the prison he allowed him first to stay out overnight and then for several nights at a time.

Soon Bunyan was regularly preaching around the villages again but always returning to the prison when the judges on Assize were expected. Then, at the end of the summer, he decided to ride down to London and visit the Independent churches there for a few days. News of this journey reached the ears of one or more of the local magistrates and they immediately thought that he must be a political agitator as well as a religious fanatic! The gaoler was severely reprimanded and was lucky not to lose his job.

Bunyan was now strictly confined and for the next seven years was not even allowed into the town or given another chance to leave the prison, although friends and relatives could occasionally visit him.

He would sit for hours at a time, studying his Bible, praying, writing several more booklets for publication and writing notes for his

Disused Baptist graveyard at Thorn near Houghton Regis. An offshoot of the Kensworth Meeting. D/E17

spiritual autobiography, *Grace Abounding* (published 1666) and his account of the physical and spiritual problems associated with his prison sentence (finally published 1765 – see above).

At other times he would take part in long and at first quite heated discussions with the other Independent Christians and Quakers who shared his cell. While they were talking he would almost unconsciously fold metal tags around a never-ending pile of boot-laces. In this way, he was able to earn a few shillings towards maintaining his wife and family.

Bunyan tries again to get a Hearing

The next meeting of the local justices was due on the 10 November 1661, but Bunyan was not called before them. When preparations began for the visit of the two judges Sir Thomas Twisden and Sir Matthew Hale, he worried in case, once again, he would be left at the prison and not get the chance to have his case brought before them. First he persuaded the gaoler to enter his name among the list of criminals who were to be called before the judges and then made sure that the sheriff knew and approved of the fact.

Unfortunately, the local magistrates heard that his name was on the list and they sent their clerk, Paul Cobb, to find the gaoler, have Bunyan's name removed from the list and make quite sure that his case did not come up. The gaoler objected because he had already written out the list, so Cobb asked for it, blotted out the gaoler's entry and wrote instead, 'That John Bunyan was committed to prison, being lawfully convicted for upholding of unlawful meetings and conventicles'.

Then to make quite sure that the judges did not send for Bunyan, he hurried to the clerk of the Assizes and warned him before reporting back to the local magistrates. Finally, he returned to the gaoler and threatened him not only with the sack but also with heavy fines if Bunyan should appear before the judges. To quote the last sentence from Bunyan's own account:

'And thus was I hindered and prevented, at that time also, from appearing before the judge, and left in prison. Farewell.'

CHAPTER SIXTEEN

The Independent Church at Bedford

During 1661 an increasing number of Independent Christians had been arrested. Local magistrates felt quite safe in keeping them in prison because a Parliamentary committee, which included Sir John Kelynge, were planning an 'Act of Uniformity'. This was finally read in the House on 14 January 1662, a week before the judges visited Bedford.

However, there were still many members of Parliament who were against a return to such a strict measure and first the Commons and then the Lords held long acrimonious debates before the bill became law on the 19 May.

Even though King Charles II had promised to protect 'tender consciences' in matters of religion he had signed the bill which required every clergyman, within the next three months, to read morning and evening prayer to his congregation and to declare before them that they accepted without reservation everything printed in the Book of Common Prayer.

Also, that every clergyman must have undergone, or now be prepared to request, ordination by a bishop. Should a minister continue to take services in a parish church without episcopal ordination, he would be liable to a heavy fine.

More than two thousand clergy, who were either not episcopally ordained or who had not made the Prayer Book declaration by 24 August, automatically lost their livings. However, Bishop Laney of Lincoln, was not too strict and only about a dozen clergymen from Bedfordshire were included. They were mainly from the north of the county; William Dell of Yeldon must have expected the summons but, on the other hand, men like James Mabbison who had been appointed to the vicarage of Roxton, by Trinity College Cambridge, during the years when ordination was not required, also had to go.

A Crowded Prison

Year by year, Bunyan continued to send petitions to the visiting judges but by the end of 1663 he must have realised he was wasting his time. Over 80 people had been brought up in front of the judges for refusing to attend church. The prison was now crowded, discipline was strict but somehow he managed to find the space and the concentration to continue writing. He published at least eight pamphlets and booklets between 1663 and 1665.

The people who were arrested for not attending church were just a small sample of the numerous protesters who were neglecting their parish churches in favour of informal services held in isolated houses and barns. John Donne who in 1662 had been ejected from the Rectory at Pertenhall, went to live at Keysoe. He held meetings there until he was arrested and sent to join Bunyan in prison.

The 'Conventicle Act'

The Act of 1664 made it possible for anyone found at one of these informal meetings to be fined £5 or to be sent to prison for three months. The second offence carried a heavier penalty and the third could result in a fine of £100 or transportation for seven years. This Act lasted for three years and John Donne was one of a small group who were actually ordered to be transported. However, possibly because the Bedfordshire magistrates disapproved of such a severe sentence, he remained in prison.

The following year 'The Five Mile Act' prevented ejected clergymen from even visiting towns or places where they had previously officiated, making it very difficult for them to earn a living. Nevertheless, in 1665 a meeting was surprised at Blunham and that year, and each of the next three, over a hundred men and women were arrested while attending such meetings.

Grace Abounding

It may have been the confusion and overcrowding that now caused the gaoler to allow Bunyan to visit his home occasionally. It was during 1666 that his spiritual autobiography *Grace Abounding To The Chief of*

Sinners was published. His visits home may have been in connection with this publication but we do not know whom he met, or whether he travelled further than the five minute walk to St Cuthbert Street. Nor do we know whether he visited any of the informal meetings or risked addressing them himself, because, for safety, the Bedford Church were no longer making entries in the church book.

It is probable that Bunyan had to return to prison during 1667 but the Conventicle Act lapsed in March 1668 and was not renewed. The Independent Christians in Bedfordshire took advantage of this and were soon meeting openly again and recruiting new members.

By the end of the year they were regularly entering reports of their business meetings and letters in their minute book. These notes included their concern about members who had ceased to attend during the recent troubles.

There were a series of discussions, days of fasting and prayer and then the decision to send two or three of the leading members to 'admonish' them and to lead them back to repentance and to readmittance of the Church. From 30 November 1668 onwards, 'Bros Bunyan' or 'John Bunyan' is often amongst those who the 'Church thought good to send'.

On 21 April 1671 he was one of a small group who sadly agreed that some of their lapsed members who refused to repent must be cut off and it is obvious that Bunyan was once more travelling all over north Bedfordshire.

The Family Reunited

After such a long absence and so much worry, Elizabeth and John must have been most relieved to be living together once more as a family.

In 1668 Mary would have been around eighteen, Elizabeth and John in their early teens and Thomas may be about ten. In addition, there was now a baby step-sister because Elizabeth's daughter, Sarah, had been born the previous year.

When John was older he set up as a brazier or 'metal man' in his own right. He is not entered as a full member of what became 'The Bunyan Meeting House' until 1693, long after his father's death. However, when his father first returned from years of sitting around in prison he was probably grateful to have a strong young man to walk or ride around the countryside with him and to do some of the journeys in his father's place. Willingly or otherwise, John must have heard his father preaching at the formal and informal gatherings that greeted them on their journeys.

Another 'Conventicle Act' is passed

Whether or not Bunyan was 'on parole' and expected to report back to the prison on a regular basis we do not know, but in Bedfordshire there was certainly a period of unwritten toleration until May 1670 when another Act of Parliament was passed forbidding both house-group and outdoor meetings. The penalties were now more in proportion to the 'crime', being mainly a series of fines but constables were allowed to actually force their way into a house if they suspected that a meeting was taking place. Also, it was possible for the magistrates to apply for help from the militia to round up suspects thought to be hiding in a wood. Worst of all, the fine would be shared with informers whose help led to an arrest and with the parish which was assumed to have suffered the loss of support from the arrested person.

Here was an excellent way of settling old scores while gaining financially and doing a service to the parish, all at the same time.

A New Threat to The Independents

Bunyan's old enemy, Dr William Foster, who was now Commissary of the Archdeacon's Court, had been infuriated to see men like Bunyan moving quite openly around the countryside. He acted straightaway, before Bunyan and his friends had realised the danger that they were in.

The very first Sunday after the passing of the Act (15 May 1670) he ordered his spies to report which house they intended to meet at. As soon as he received a message that they were at the house of John Fenn, the hat manufacturer, right in the centre of the town, he issued a warrant and sent the constable round to arrest everyone present in the house. The preacher was Nehemiah Cox, a respected shoemaker and son of Benjamin Cox, who, like Edward Harrison of Kensworth, had retired from his parish church (in Devon) before the Civil War. Also like Harrison, he had come to believe that only those who chose to be baptised when they were old enough to make a responsible choice, should be allowed to receive communion.

A group meeting in the house of John Fenn and with such a preacher was just what Foster needed for a 'show trial'. Cox was sent to prison 'for speaking seditious words'. He made no attempt to appease the magistrate and even said that he considered the Established Church to be anti-Christian.

The Collection of Fines

One of the churchwardens from St Paul's, the parish in which the meeting had been held, was ordered to collect fines from the 28 people found in the house. John Bunyan was not one of them but an anonymous writer wrote a pamphlet to describe the efforts of the friends and neighbours of the accused to prevent the collection of fines.

The churchwarden, Thomas Battison, went to the yard of John Bardolf, a respected maltster but he had sold or hidden his stock. As

Bronze doors at the Bunyan Meeting Free Church, Bedford.

Battison was discussing with his assistants what they should do, a crowd gathered and while the more educated men held his attention trying to argue with him, the crowd got increasingly rowdy and were delighted when someone managed to pin a calf's tail to his coat!

He managed to escape the crowd and went to collect five shillings from the nearby grocer, Edward Coventon. Coventon was not a poor man but he refused on principle to pay the fine. While they argued one of his men brought out a big brass kettle and Battison decided to take that instead. However the crowd had caught up with him and he could not walk through the streets carrying the kettle, so he paid a boy sixpence to take it to a nearby inn. Part of the now extremely noisy crowd followed Battison and others followed the boy. The inn-keeper refused to admit the boy or the kettle and placed it in the road outside his gates.

By this time the crowd were so noisy and unruly that Battison feared for his safety and returned home. The next day was market day and there would be even more people assembled in the centre of town, so the magistrates ordered the parish constable and some members of the militia to accompany him.

Bardolf's malthouse was in the yard of one of the inns situated actually in the market place but the presence of the soldiers made it possible for the malthouse doors to be forced and fourteen quarters of malt to be loaded on a cart and removed.

Some of the members must have got together and discussed what they should do. Nobody wanted Bunyan to be sent back to prison unnecessarily so the others acted without him; on the following Sunday morning they again met at John Fenn's house. Battison arrived at about nine o'clock and ordered the group to depart and when they refused sent to Dr Foster for advice. He supplied a list of names of men who would help with the arrests. Battison patiently went from house to house watched by a crowd of about a hundred spectators.

Within an hour they had rounded up all the members of the group and they took them to the Swan Hotel. At four o'clock they were released with their fines doubled.

Poor Thomas Battison spent several days of the following week accompanied by William Foster and protected by soldiers as he tried to collect goods from the accused, who again refused to pay the fines. They took three cart loads of wood from Thomas Cooper, who made wooden heels for the shoemaker, leaving him with no way of supporting his family and other wood was taken from Thomas Arthur the pipe maker. However, they obviously decided not to touch the evil-smelling skins of Daniel Rich, the tanner, whose wife had been at the meeting, and instead, took his best coat. They then collected goods from Mr Jay the baker and all the tools, even the anvil, from Mr Isaac, the blacksmith.

Passive Resistance

Foster was obviously worried at the levity of the townspeople and the contempt of the offenders so he decided to make an example of a wealthy widow, Mary Tilney. She had been fined £20, an exceptionally heavy fine under the new legislation. He decided to accompany Battison, the constable and the soldiers, on their visit to Mrs Tilney's house. As he went along he tried to impress passers-by to come and help but by this time everyone knew what was going on and each one, in turn, found some good excuse to refuse. Foster then sent messages to various workmen to come and help him, most of whom also refused.

By the time they arrived at Mrs Tilney's house Foster was extremely angry and Mrs Tilney had had plenty of warning to hide any possessions of particularly high value. The result was that they stripped her house of furniture and even took the sheets from her bed.

The next day, when Foster and his procession appeared on the streets, the people of Bedford were prepared. Before the messengers arrived to summon them to assist, they had closed their businesses, taken their families and work-people with them and left for the country. The news spread that many shops and business houses were closing for the day and when Foster arrived in the market place it was to find the town deserted as though it were a holiday.

The unknown pamphleteer included a passage about passive resistance that Mrs Brittain* compares with the policy of Mahatma Gandhi or Aldous Huxley.

In the presence of the Justice of the Peace the fine meted out to Thomas Archer the pipe-maker had been raised from goods worth £6 to goods worth £11 because he had locked the door against the officers. Mrs Tilney's fine had originally been £20 and the quantity of goods

In The Steps of John Bunyan.

taken was worth more than double that amount. On the following day, Battison, his constables and soldiers solemnly marched up the High Street, trying to ignore the jeering and shouting from either side and went to collect a fine of £5 from John Fenn, the hatter; there were 29 hats in the shop and he took them all. Then, following the example of the justice, he came back with a cart and removed all Fenn's furniture. Then he did the same at the shop and house of Samuel Fenn, John Fenn's brother.

Once they had completed their rounds in Bedford they moved out to Cardington where they removed a farmer's cows and stripped a weaver's house and workshop. The latter was not only penniless but quite unable to support himself. He and his wife were obliged to leave the village.

The Brave Men and Women of Bedford

The anonymous pamphleteer published his account the following year and some time later Foster replied. Thanks to the surviving pamphlets in the Bodleian Library, Oxford, we know the names and histories of a handful of people who stood firm regardless of personal loss.

During the reign of Queen Mary, several major landowners from Bedfordshire and roundabout, spent time in Calvinist Geneva and during the religious persecution which led up to the Civil War they were reluctant to mete out serious punishment to men whose only 'crime' was to desire freedom of worship. By 1670, many of these 'tolerant' men had been replaced and there was less sympathy with the Independents. Several Bedfordshire men were sentenced to transportation, although the sentences were not carried out. It may be that Bunyan's writing and his wide popularity saved him from a similar sentence. The news that the popular preacher, author of *Grace Abounding* and of many pamphlets, was to be transported might have caused many waverers to stand out against the Act of Parliament and those who were responsible for it.

John Bunyan was not connected with the above events but they are an example of the risks that a handful of people were prepared to take in Bedford and illustrate what was going on all over Bedfordshire and in many other counties.

CHAPTER SEVENTEEN

The Pilgrim's Progress

Within weeks of the passing of the new Act, John Bunyan was returned to prison. The things that he had seen and heard in the last few months and the pamphlets which he had read, both for and against the Established Church, had caused him much concern. Back in prison he again had time to sit and think – and to write about his thoughts.

With his own grown up children in mind and those of his friends he had for some time been writing a story about a pilgrim who set out on a long journey in search of salvation.

By making his hero a pilgrim who was undertaking a journey, he was able to use quite simple language and to introduce his readers gradually to all sorts of difficult situations that they would meet through life's journey and, above all, the different types of people they would meet along the way. Some of these people would deliberately try to mislead them, others, for a variety of reasons, would offer them easy solutions or try to persuade them to give up halfway.

Although this, his most famous book, was not published until 1678, his biographers think that he wrote it over a period of several years. He was not an educated man in the formal sense of the word and must, at times, have had great difficulty trying to understand the pamphlets and letters which were either written against views that he himself had expressed, or which were written to advertise views which he felt were misleading or downright dangerous. After hours of struggling to put into words his objections to these pamphlets or to write down for others the results of his Bible study and prayer, how relaxing it must have been to sit and dream about his days walking the roads of Bedfordshire and Hertfordshire. If his over-taxed brain and the noise and smell of his fellow prisoners prevented him from dropping off to sleep, he could follow an imaginary journey as he walked out from

The window, in Elstow Church, commemorating The Holy War. F9
Right: *The Pilgrim window, Harlington while under repair.* F14

Elstow; stopping to chat with other travellers or, very quietly, following footpaths across country, noting the first flowers, nesting birds or frog spawn, after a long cold winter.

Once he had had the idea of starting Christian off on his pilgrimage, he could get his ideas straight in his own head by letting Christian, his hero, engage in a series of conversations with the very people whose views he was trying to deny.

The Vicar of Northill

Early in 1671, the vicar of Northill, Edward Fowler, published a book entitled, *The Design of Christianity*. He came from a family of men who had stood out against the Established Church and he himself had originally been a campaigner for freedom of worship. However, when the Act of Uniformity was passed in 1662, he like so many others had accepted the Book of Common Prayer.

Aь the years had gone by he had so far persuaded himself that he had done the right thing that he published this book which caused Bunyan so much anger and distress. Sitting in prison, Bunyan had ample time to prepare an argument against Fowler's book but to put his arguments down on paper was not easy for this inspired preacher. He studied the book sentence by sentence but never really understood Fowler's argument. Nevertheless, he eventually managed to write his reply* to the man who was prepared to give up, among other things, his belief in freedom of worship in return for his freedom, a comfortable house and a congenial way of living.

The Story of 'Mr By-ends'

Instead of writing a point-by-point debate Bunyan turned to colourful examples: it was much easier to write about Mr By-ends and his relatives Lord Turn-about, Lord Time-server, Lord Fail-speech, Mr Facing-both-ways, Mr Any-thing; and the parson, Mr Two-tongues.

Then, remembering his fishing trips at Bedford where he watched the boatmen navigating the River Ouse, he mentions By-end's great grandfather, a water man who looked one way while rowing in the other. By-ends had got most of his estate by working in the same way!

By-ends explains to Christian:

> It is true we somewhat differ in religion from those of the strictest sort, yet but in two small points:– first, we never strive against the wind and tide; secondly, we are always most zealous when religion goes in his silver slippers; we love much to walk with him in the street, if the sun shines and the people applaud him.

When Christian asks him how he came to get his name, By-ends explains that he has been lucky always to 'jump in my judgement with the present way of the times, whatever it was . . .'. If he was obliged to change then he would find a way to count that change a blessing and not allow malicious people to load him with reproach.

How much more effective to let Christian and Mr By-ends put their arguments in the simple language used by children.

A Defence of the Doctrine of Justification by Faith in Jesus Christ. A Reply to Edward Fowler. Published 1672.

Fool's gold, found at Pulloxhill may have inspired the 'Hill of Lucre' mentioned in The Pilgrim's Progress. F/G14

Christian tells By-ends that if he wishes to accompany them on their journey he will have to go against the wind and tide, and also, 'own religion' (admit to being a member, or a believer) not just when it was acceptably dressed in silver slippers, but also when others shunned it because it was dressed in rags. He must be prepared to be seen to be a friend of religion, not just when it was greeted by applause but also when it was imprisoned and dragged an iron ball. By-ends, of course, goes off on his own and when Christian looks back he is concerned to see how many other travellers followed him.

What a wonderful way this was to pour scorn on a man who he felt had given up his unpopular beliefs to save his living and his way of life. Of course, this method of prose doesn't allow for deep discussion as to whether a man who gives up part of the things that he holds dearly can do more good by continuing to hold office than by being incarcerated in prison.

This is an idea which people have been obliged to come to terms with throughout the centuries. The very fact that Christian abandoned his wife and children because his wife was too nervous and apprehensive to accompany him, has put some people off the whole of Christian's journey.

The Pastor

When John Gifford was approaching death, back in 1655, he had foreseen that his beloved 'church' could be split asunder by the clash of personalities who held deeply-felt views which differed from those of other members of the group. He foresaw a situation where adults, and had previously been baptised as children, might insist that all believers must be baptised again as adults but others might not think this necessary for church members and either form a breakaway movement or refuse to join the church altogether. He advised that adult baptism should not be a condition of membership and the group agreed. Nevertheless, it was a point which sometimes threatened to cause trouble and Bunyan planned to write a book of explanation.* Gifford also begged them not to cause dissent when electing a new leader. On that occasion Oliver Cromwell had helped them to select John Burton and, as Burton had died just before the Restoration and the break up of the church at St John's, it had been a suitable arrangement for John Whiteman, a Cardington farmer, and Samuel Fenn, a Bedford hat maker, to share the difficult position. Between them they tried to help and encourage the scattered members both those in Bedford and out in the villages.

Although Bunyan was obliged to remain in prison throughout most of 1671, changes were going on. Locally, both Lord Chief Justice Kelynge and Giles Thorne, who as Archdeacon of Bedford had harrassed the Independent Christians, died. Nationally, King Charles II was trying to find a way of rescuing his Roman Catholic friends from the same laws which imprisoned Bunyan and prevented 'non-conforming' ministers like William Dell from holding a church living. This one-time Rector of Yeldon had died in 1690 and by his own wishes had been buried in a small wood not far from where Bunyan had first been arrested.

King Charles realised that the majority of Parliamentary members still wanted the Established Church to be supported by legislation but it was known publicly that he was trying to find a way around the

Differences in Judgement about Water Baptism – No Bar to Communion Published 1673.

impasse. If the King was in favour of relaxing the law then the Bedford officials could also be somewhat more lenient and so, well before Christmas, Bunyan was home once more.

Whiteman and Fenn had not had an easy time encouraging and supporting their scattered band. Although they were in as much risk as any of the others and Fenn was actually imprisoned at one stage, they did not get unanimous support and, despite the difficulties they were in, some of the members continued to dispute points of religion.

When Bunyan had been 'unofficially free' and spending time at home during the previous year, some members had wanted to offer him the position of Pastor but his return to prison had prevented it. However, the removal of tension during the winter of 1671 made them think that he would soon be officially set free.

At a General Assembly of the Independent Church, held at Haynes towards the end of November, the matter was discussed and members were asked to include the subject in their prayers. It was discussed again at a Bedford meeting on the last day of the year and special meetings were arranged at Bedford, Haynes and Gamlingay and then on 21 January 1672 a General Assembly was held at Bedford and after a show of hands, the congregation did, 'Call forth and appoint our brother John Bunyan to the pastorall office or eldership. And he accepting thereof, gave up himself to serve Christ and his Church in that charge; and received of the Elders the right hand of fellowship.'

As a sign of their respect and affection for John Fenn, the congregation elected him a deacon and put him in charge of their money and the care of the poor. Finally, they elected a committee of seven men who included John Fenn and Nehemiah Cox to help Bunyan with his work in the surrounding villages.

A 'Declaration of Indulgence'

King Charles eventually decided to use the royal prerogative to suspend the laws which had so repressed the Independent Church. On 8 May John Bunyan, John Fenn and several others sent a petition to the King. The circumstances of their arrest were confirmed by the sheriff and their official pardon was issued on 13 September.

The Declaration also allowed organised groups of christians, who did not wish to attend the Church of England, to register their own place of public worship. Mr Crompton, the Elstow magistrate who had considered bailing Bunyan back in 1660, now sold Josias Ruffhead an orchard and barn in Mill Lane, Bedford. The barn was then licensed as a place of worship and on 20 August Ruffhead transferred the barn and orchard to Bunyan and the committee. The description of the exact location, gives a good picture of 17th-century Bedford,

> on a strip of land between Castle Lane and Mill Lane or School Lane on the south and north, and between a garden held by John Eston, on the east side (with a barn upon it) called Pynners, and a garden with a dovehouse upon it on the west side, still held by Josias Ruffhead, and separated by a paling.

The strip of land may have been part of the moat which remained from the dismantling of the castle in 1224. The present meeting house, which was built in 1850, is very near the castle mound.

In May 1672, Bunyan applied for a licence to preach and for other licences for 25 other preachers and 30 other buildings; 19 in Bedfordshire, three in Northamptonshire, three in Buckinghamshire, two in Cambridgeshire and one in Hertfordshire. This included John Allen to preach at the house of Widow Reade in Stevington and Carlton.

'Bishop' Bunyan and his Travels

Some writers have given Bunyan the nickname 'Bishop'. This is hardly surprising as he frequently travelled around these churches and is recorded as also visiting Leicester.

Some churches he visited quite regularly, especially those in and around North Bedfordshire. During one journey in February 1674 an incident occurred which gave his enemies the chance to cause scandal. There was a family called Beaumont who lived at Edworth on the Hertfordshire county boundary. They had often attended meetings of the Independent Church and John Beaumont had been an admirer of Bunyan until he was influenced against the Independents by a neighbour.

However, his daughter, Agnes, joined the church at Gamlingay, a branch of the Bedford church, and it was Bunyan who was the pastor on the night that she became a member. Knowing that Bunyan would be preaching on that particular Sunday, she was very anxious to attend. However, the man who was supposed to give her a ride into Gamlingay on his horse failed to turn up and as Bunyan approached she ran out and begged him to allow her to ride with him on his horse. Her brother and his wife were going in on their horse and they all thought that the obvious answer was for her to travel with Bunyan.

This was quite normal behaviour in the 17th century, especially when the roads were a sea of mud, but John Beaumont was now aggressively against the Independents, especially Bunyan. As the last thing that Bunyan wanted was to get involved in a family quarrel, he agreed reluctantly, but unfortunately Beaumont came back from the fields in time to see them riding away together.

When Agnes returned home, he had locked her out; he shouted through the door that he would not let her in until she promised never to attend the Gamlingay meeting again. Poor Agnes spent the night in the barn and the next five nights in her brother's house but knowing that her father would never give in she returned home on the following Sunday and did not go to church. Then, on the Tuesday, to her complete horror, her father fell to the floor. She stood staring down at him and gradually realised that he was dead.

An Anglican clergyman from Bedford had seen Bunyan riding with Agnes and began to spread rumours in Baldock market. This was the same day that her father died and gossip began to spread. Some months previously she had refused to marry a local lawyer and now he saw his chance to get his own back and spread the rumour that she had poisoned her father. There was a dreadful scandal and the clergyman delayed the funeral until an investigation proved her innocence. Agnes recovered from the unpleasantness and in 1720 was buried in the Tilehouse Street graveyard in Hitchin, another church which Bunyan used to visit.

Bunyan, however, had quite innocently given his enemies cause to create scandal and there were always people watching out to cause trouble. This was particularly embarrassing because one of the more painful parts of his work and one in which he was particularly patient was checking up on and trying to reform other members who got into trouble in the community.

The Meeting Houses lose their Licences

Bunyan continued to travel over a very wide area although after one year King Charles had been forced to withdraw his Declaration of Indulgence. There was an uneasy peace while Charles and Parliament debated the subject. Although there were no arrests, no more meeting places were licensed after February 1673.

Despite all his travelling, Bunyan managed to continue writing but mainly on things concerning matters that were relevant at that time. His story about Christian's journey was left on the shelf. Then, in February 1675, everything changed again; conventicles were again illegal; licences for their meeting houses were withdrawn.

Bunyan heard from a sympathiser that a warrant had been prepared for his arrest (it was dated 4 March 1675) authorising the Bedford constables to arrest him if he was caught preaching.

For eighteen months he managed to avoid arrest, if he went preaching it was at unexpected times and places; he must not be caught flagrantly breaking the law. The fine for anyone caught preaching was £20 for the first offence and £40 for the second. Bunyan knew only too well that if he didn't pay the fine, the church-wardens would once more remove not only his furniture but his anvil and his tools.

Elizabeth was still spending a great deal of time without him while he went on his travels but he could at least support them financially and be at home if she seriously needed him.

She still had some of her step-children at home and her own two children, Sarah aged seven in 1675 and a three-year-old son called Joseph. Bunyan must try and avoid another spell in prison.

He managed to get three more booklets finished and published during 1675, possibly because he was forced to spend more time at home.

He continued writing and in 1676 published *The Strait Gate* a pamphlet which emphasised the difficulty of passing through this life with all its wordly temptations and still being in an acceptable state to pass through St Luke's 'strait gate'* at one's end. There are themes in this very serious piece of writing, which he developed in a lighter but much clearer way in *The Pilgrim's Progress*.

Imprisoned Again

The warrant which was prepared in 1675 was never used. The Bedford

---

*St Luke's Gospel Chapter 13, Verse 24.

Millbrook gorge may have inspired 'The Valley of the Shadow' in The Pilgrim's Progress. E11

church went 'underground' and no longer entered their meetings in the Minute Book.

However, the Commissary, Dr William Foster, was determined to get Bunyan back into prison. He remembered how the original charge had been made and summoned Bunyan before the Archdeacon's Court to answer a charge from the church-wardens at St Cuthbert's that he refused to attend the parish church or take communion.

Bunyan ignored the summons and was excommunicated in his absence. This had happened to several of the local Independents and there had been no further action but in Bunyan's case when notification was sent to the bishop, Dr Foster arranged with the sheriff for Bunyan's arrest. On 21 June, 1677, Bunyan was returned to prison.

Once again he had time to write. During his period of freedom he had realised that 'sin' was still one of the biggest hurdles that came between a man and his salvation.

Everywhere he went to preach crowds turned up to listen to him. They were interested, they were often enthusiastic, they asked questions and listened to his answers but when it came to making a personal commitment to Christ something held them back. When he talked to them afterwards they appeared to believe in every word he said and yet something made them feel that all he had said applied to other people, not to them.

He could still remember all too painfully his own years of misery and he sat for days at a time trying to put his thoughts and experiences down on paper*.

'When all refuge fails' he wrote 'and a man is made to see that there is nothing left him but sin, death and damnation unless he flies to Christ for Life; then he flies, and not till then.'

It was a very difficult subject to write about; a very difficult message to put across when the person that one was trying to convince was not there to spell out his doubts for himself.

Bunyan's fears and nightmares had started in childhood; could he try and help other children through these terrible doubts and confusions?

The Pilgrim's Progress is Published

Bunyan's friends and family were allowed to visit and no doubt members of his church committee brought their problems to him. It may have been the frustration in trying to help sufferers through a third person or through a written sermon that encouraged Bunyan to show his church friends pages from his pilgrim's journey and to query whether they thought this a better way of helping some of their less educated companions.

Although one or two people were doubtful, maybe thinking it to be irreverent or worrying that adult men and women might feel they were being treated as children, the majority surprised Bunyan by their enthusiasm. This must be published as soon as possible; it could help all manner of people, including those who did not get the chance to discuss their worries with people of like mind. A book like this did not need a guide or an interpreter, it took serious themes and messages straight to the reader in his own home.

Bunyan was still undecided but in the end he made a selection of Christian's adventures and published them on 18 February 1678 with a long introduction or apology in which he describes how difficult it

Come and Welcome to Jesus Christ, published 1678.

The Swan Inn at Elstow. F9

was for him to give the casting vote as to whether or not his story was suitable for publication.

'Now was I in a strait, and did not see which was the best thing to be done by me: At last I thought; since you are thus divided, I print it will; and so the case decided.'

The book was an instant success, was reprinted within a few months, and again the following year. Some of Christian's other adventures were then inserted, including his meeting with Mr By-ends*.

*There is a detailed account of the many different versions included in *John Bunyan* by John Brown M.A.

When *The Pilgrim's Progress* was first published in 1678 it was sold at one shilling and sixpence (7½p) per copy. By the time that Bunyan died, ten years later 12 editions had been printed amounting to a hundred thousand copies. In addition it was translated into French, Dutch and Welsh. It has now been translated into over two hundred languages and dialects. There are copies of the book in 168 different languages and dialects in the Bunyan Meeting Museum in Mill Street, Bedford.

When one of the only four known copies of the first edition was auctioned in 1926 it was eventually sold for £6,800.

The stream which still runs under Stevington Church appears as a small pool and may have been the place which inspired 'The Holy Well' of The Pilgrim's Progress. D6

CHAPTER EIGHTEEN

John Bunyan's Later Writings

Bunyan had been able to take his manuscript up to his London publisher in December 1677 knowing that at last he could travel freely about the country. Before the publication of *The Pilgrim's Progress*, he was alraedy well known and respected among the London Independents. On 21 June two of the more senior members had signed a bond, guaranteeing his good behaviour and in a surprisingly short time he was released. However, the political situation was still very insecure and the informer, Titus Oates, stirred up trouble in London and led many people to think that not conforming to the established church might lead to treason. The Bedford church was able to meet once more and from time-to-time made entries in their minute book but Bunyan had been released on a bond guaranteeing his good, i.e. conforming, behaviour and was obliged to refrain from playing a leading role in its affairs.

Nevertheless, he could enjoy family life once again in the St Cuthbert Street cottage with Elizabeth and the younger children, Sarah and Joseph. Maybe, the restrictions which prevented him travelling for days at a time as a preacher, gave him the opportunity to continue writing.

He was concerned about the wickedness that he saw all around him. Not just in prison but in the towns and villages through which he travelled and even within his own church. He could understand the attitude that if something was 'socially acceptable' then it was easy for any individual to find an excuse for bad behaviour. If an army officer used the name of God as a swear word how could you expect a common soldier to do any different? If a landowner or a businessman cheated others or ran up debts, how could you convince a small shopkeeper or craftsman that it was not just damaging to the customer but also damaging to themselves? Drunkenness and gambling were not just damaging to one's health and one's pocket and, of course, to one's family but above all to one's immortal soul. First he published *Welcome To Jesus* begging his readers to confess their sins, accept the loving forgiveness that was offered and to begin their lives anew. Then he followed it with *A Treatise Of The Fear Of God* trying to make his readers face up to the awareness of God's anger towards those who refused the salvation offered.

Writing these type of sermons, when your congregation were scattered and in their own homes, was far more difficult than discussing problems face to face. Maybe this was why he decided to write his next book as a series of conversations.

The Life and Death of Mr Badman

In 1678 he published a book which he described as *A Familiar Dialogue Between Mr Wiseman and Mr Attentive.*

In his opening letter to the reader he explains that, as *The Pilgrim's Progress* had proved acceptable to so many, it had occurred to him that it might be helpful to set out the dangers of loose living in the form of a dialogue. It is a conversation between two men: Mr Wiseman describes the life of a boy that he has known from childhood and the bad behaviour of that person throughout; Mr Attentive cannot wait to cut in with examples of other people that he has known who behaved in a similar way or who met a similar fate. The main character discussed by Mr Wiseman comes from a good home with caring parents who do everything possible to set a good example. When they fail to influence or control the boy they choose a master to whom they can apprentice him. They know that this master will constantly set him a good example and try to control what they hope is just his boyish thoughtlessness.

In fact this obnoxious young person ignores all the help offered, embraces every sin he can find, damages everybody who tries to help him and leads as many other people into wickedness as he can persuade to follow him.

It is not an easy book to read; each 'episode' is wrapped up in biblical references which is confusing for a modern reader. Taken separately, the incidents would make the basis for a set of sermons to be used today or in any century or could be used as material for a late night television serial.

While writing this book, Bunyan has unintentionally given us a wealth of detail concerning life in 17th-century England. In his opening letter, Bunyan wrote:

> ... yet have I as little as may be gone out of the road of mine own observation of things. Yea, I think I may truly say that to the best of my remembrance, all the things that here I discourse of, I mean as to matter of fact, have been acted upon the stage of this world, even many times before mine eyes.

We get simple little stories which may well be from his own childhood of boys scrumping apples, boys swearing as a form of bravado to outdo each other and of boys not wanting to go to church or read the Bible. However, when he gets on to describing the sins of adulthood, he draws on his experiences as a travelling craftsman, as a soldier and as a preacher, responsible for the spiritual well-being of his scattered congregation.

He describes the downfall of the habitual drinker and how his behaviour affects his family and those round about. From this sin he moves on to describe various circumstances whereby men either visited prostitutes or, worse still, persuaded married ladies or innocent girls, to commit sin for the men's pleasure. Some of the incidents mentioned appear to be cautionary tales which were in general circulation at the time. There was a tale told about a lady from Derbyshire who, when accused of petty theft, wished the ground to swallow her up should she be guilty and who was then drawn into the ground up to her waist by a form of dry whirlpool. Then, before her friends could help her, a great stone fell and cracked open her skull and knocked her into the ground. The surrounding soil completely covered her and her dead body was eventually recovered four yards below the surface.

Mr Wiseman's advice to parents who had a son who was out of control was to mix 'their merceries with loving rebukes and their loving rebukes with fatherly and motherly compassions...' He appreciated how desperate parents were to save their children from hell but assured them that they were more likely to do good through love, 'than by being cherlish and severe towards them...'

Bunyan's two characters go on to discuss deception in business from the point of view of the staff, the owner, the customer, the creditor and the bankrupt. They discuss marriage and the depths to which men would sink to try to ensnare a wealthy wife, followed by the heartless way they then treated the ladies.

From this, Bunyan introduces a subject of which he had recent personal knowledge; men who disapproved of their wives attending the Independent churches and, as a result, reported these meetings to the authorities.

Under the subject of pride, Bunyan was able to introduce people who attended worship, 'so decked and bedaubed with their fangles and toys' and with their faces covered in paint. Between them, these two men manage to discuss a very wide range of worldly sins that might attract a man at different stages of his life. Mr Wiseman points out numerous biblical references concerning these sins, and they discuss between them how easily a socially accepted misdemeanour can lead to a soul-destroying sin and also lead other people to the same terrible end. Finally, they discuss repentance at different stages of a man's life and the foolishness, if not wickedness, of leaving this to one's dying hours.

The Holy War

Although 17th-century readers were more used to books that had numerous biblical references and which had, therefore, a rather more disjointed style than we would find acceptable, they did not find the experiences of Mr Badman as compelling as those of Christian in *The Pilgrim's Progress*. Christian's journey was a series of adventures and he met several interesting characters who helped to break up the repetitive listing of the snares set out along life's journey. The 'message' was thickly enveloped in a contemporary adventure story which was set in a wholly familiar landscape.

Mr Badman and his friend made no journey; they sat under a tree, and the entire book is one long conversation between two men. Although it did not have the amazing sales of *The Pilgrim's Progress* it was well received within the Independent Church. Bunyan had the satisfaction of knowing that it would be widely read by those for whom it was intended; the individual Christians struggling with life's temptations and those men, like himself, but perhaps without his experiences or sympathy in teaching, who were called upon to strengthen and advise their weaker brethren. By the time that Mr Badman was in circulation he was already planning his next book.

King Charles II was finding it increasingly difficult to rule the country. The people of England still wanted a King but were becoming alarmed to find that King Charles II was repeating the mistakes of his father. Unfortunately, the King accepted the advice of an inner circle who favoured direct rule and encouraged him to act without the consent of Parliament.

Living in the county town of Bedford, Bunyan must have been aware of the political confusion within both local and national government. He would have heard people discussing the possibility that King Charles, if thwarted by the Bedford Corporation, might have the elected burgesses removed and others, recommended to him by his friend, the Earl of Ailesbury (from Houghton House), put into the Corporation in their place.* Bunyan began to toy with the idea of publicising his message; that both young and old, weak and strong, were continually under attack, not so much from violence and force but from persuasion and temptation.

The Pilgrim's Progress, with its strong story line had reached a wider readership than Mr Badman, which was restricted to a single, drawn-out conversation. Due to circumstances beyond his control Bunyan had plenty of time, why not try another story? He decided to use as his central theme, a town under attack from the various forces of evil. He had experience of war and war-time situations; he knew the temptations that soldiers faced when they were away from home. He may not have had personal experience of setting up, living through or of breaking a siege, but he had lived for some years in the garrison at Newport Pagnell and his friends had marched out to help with siege breaking.

For two years he wrote and re-wrote his script, which was published in 1682 as *The Holy War*. The adventure side of the 'War' must not be allowed to overrule his main purpose which was to portray the fight between the forces of good and of evil, to gain possession of a human soul.

He named his town 'Mansoul' (the soul of man) and gave it five gates which the attackers could use as the potential weak points in its defence. These were: Ear-gate, Eye-gate, Mouth-gate, Nose-gate and Feel-gate; the mayor of the town was 'Lord Understanding'. One of the most senior positions in 17th-century local government was that of 'Recorder' and Bunyan's Recorder was called 'Conscience'. (The

*This did indeed happen in 1684.

Deputy Recorder of Bedford, had recently stood out against the Earl of Ailesbury and even King Charles himself, rather than act against his conscience).

This then was the town, or rather the soul, which was under attack. As he draws on his experiences as an itinerant worker and as a soldier to help give body to his basic sermon, this should have been as exciting 'a read' for the 17th-century book buyer as was *The Pilgrim's Progress*. However, by the time he had finished, he had fallen between the two basic methods that he had previously used. Mr Badman had far less story line than *The Pilgrim's Progress* but its very tightness of structure allowed a great many sins to be discussed without causing confusion. *The Pilgrim's Progress* had such a strong story line that the reader's attention was not allowed to wander. However, *The Holy War* got out of control. One message led to another; the mention of a sin caused him to desert the story line and chase off after the implications of that sin.

The Town of 'Mansoul'

A certain King Shaddai built himself a town, called 'Mansoul', for his own pleasure; it had an ideal climate and situation with, on the whole, a delightful population, although between them the people had a mixture of the usual weaknesses of character and minor failings. The town was defended by strong walls so that no invaders could gain entrance unless the townspeople decided of their own free will to let them in.

Outside the town lived 'Diabolus' 'a great and mighty prince and yet poor and beggarly'. Diabolus, of course, turned out to be the invader who had no real need to break down the defensive walls to gain entrance. By tactical use of the Ear-Gate and Eye-Gate he had soon seduced a large number of the inhabitants. Then he sounded a trumpet outside the strongest wall and talked persuasively to the civic leaders while one of his officers managed to kill 'Captain Resistance'. The 'battle' was over; the gates were opened and the people invited him and his supporters into the town. Once inside and in control, like George Orwell's 20th-century pigs in *Animal Farm*, they defaced the very image of the previous leader, so that he was soon forgotten.

While Bunyan was writing this book, King Charles II dissolved Parliament and once more caused one group of landowners to be suspicious of another. There was tension in both town and country and

Bunyan again witnessed examples of men who changed sides for money or preferment; worse still, who were sometimes obliged to change sides or lose their jobs.

The Story of *The Holy War*

'Conscience', the fictional Recorder, was one of the only officers of Mansoul Corporation to stand out against Diabolus, but both he and the mayor were soon discredited and lost their influence. Lord Lustings became the new mayor and Mr Forget-good, judge. Among other officials were Mr Incredulity, Mr Haughty, Mr Swearing, Mr Whoring, Mr Pitiless, Mr Drunkenness and Mr Atheism.

King Shaddai (God?) had been away at the time of the attack and when he and his son, Prince Emmanuel (Jesus?), heard about the way their poor town was faring under Diabolus (the Devil?), they were very distressed. However, they never gave up hope of winning back the town.

A Topical Tale

More than a year before King Charles II demanded that the people of Bedford should exchange their ancient character for a new, inferior one, Diabolus had made such a demand from Mansoul. Just as the people of Bedford would in the future really be tricked and coerced into giving way, so the fictional people of Mansoul surrendered. Encouraged by this, Diabolus sent 'Mr Filth' around the streets issuing licences which not only permitted the receiver to behave with uncontrolled lust but also forbade any of their neighbours or friends to try to curb their behaviour.

To help them defend themselves, he provided breastplates which would harden their hearts, and shields which would strengthen unbelief. To those who wanted them he even offered helmets, which would reassure the wearer that salvation is available as an automatic right and does not have to be earned.

Throughout this story there are several details which strengthen our belief that Bunyan had previously served in Cromwell's army. The soldiers of Prince Emmanuel crossed the countryside without ever robbing the villagers of food and supplies, King Shaddai having

Stevington Cross where Bunyan used to preach. D6

provided sufficient food. When they arrive at Mansoul, Prince Emmanuel tried to avoid killing civilians by first sending his captains to try to persuade the people verbally to transfer their loyalty back to their King. Only when that failed did he mount a siege.

It dragged on all the summer with the people of Mansoul trying to bargain a compromise with Emmanuel, who refused to accept lowered standards, or half-hearted promises. Eventually, the prince got control of the town and punishment was meted out depending on the knowledge or the willingness with which the sins had been committed.

However, this wasn't the end of the story. Bunyan had not found a slot for many of the spiritual and moral arguments that he wanted to introduce and so the story line was revived. Other characters were introduced and the unfortunate residents of Mansoul were dragged, willingly or unwillingly, through yet more adventures.

The Holy War was published in 1682 but even by 17th-century standards it was difficult to read. Remove three-quarters of the spiritual discussion and it might, like *The Pilgrim's Progress*, have been a readable allegory, enjoyed by a fairly wide section of the population. On the other hand, remove the story and, as in the dialogue between Mr Wiseman and Mr Attentive it might have found praise within the Independent Church. As it is, the story is too deeply buried in the spiritual arguments and the arguments are too confused to be followed by any but the most experienced reader.

Maybe if it had been understood by a wider readership it might have landed Bunyan in yet more trouble. Not just because his Prince Emmanuel was supported by an army which was recognisably Parliamentary but also because so much of the practical side of his allegory came true in the years following publication!

King Charles II withdraws Bedford's Ancient Charter

First, several Bedford officials were removed from the ruling body, 'The Corporation', and during the winter of 1683 the Earl of Ailesbury managed to get over 70 of his supporters admitted as burgesses in the town, even though some of them had no connection with its affairs.

Then, King Charles, through the Earl of Ailesbury, set out to get complete control over the town. He requested the return of their ancient charter which gave them freedom to elect their own council, the 'Corporation', and promised another, similar charter in return.

When their mayor, Paul Cobb (the clerk who had debated with Bunyan when he was first imprisoned) protested to the Earl, he wrote a most sympathetic letter, promising to make everything easy for the town; the cost would be negligible and his own solicitor would act for them. Then the Earl set out to win over Paul Cobb, the mayor, by offering to arrange an opportunity for him to be presented to King Charles. This of course, would take place when he brought the charter to London.

The Earl of Ailesbury outwits Bedford

When the charters had been exchanged, the Earl of Ailesbury, in a truly *Animal Farm* situation, rode into Bedford accompanied by more than five hundred people who in misplaced jubilation had ridden out to meet him near Elstow. Thus they escorted and gave homage to a new charter which in return for two new fairs each year gave King Charles complete control over their governing council. He could 'hire and fire' any member of the Corporation, that he wished. On arrival at the Guildhall, the Earl read out the charter and quickly went on to praise King Charles and admonish his listeners as to how lucky they were to have such a gracious and generous King.

The church bells rang out to welcome the damaging charter; there was a banquet for those invited into the Guildhall and free beer outside for those who weren't.

The mayor thanked the Earl for honouring them with his presence and sent thanks and messages of loyalty to the King. Because of the persuasive skills of the Earl and his assistants, the problem of raising the money to cover the cost of this damaging charter caused more bitterness within the Corporation than the charter itself. However, nobody saw the similarity of this piece of brain washing and the way that Diabolus and his assistants behaved at Mansoul.

Into Hiding

It was just as well that *The Holy War* did not add to the problems of John Bunyan and his Independent Church. During the years since his release from prison, Bunyan had been travelling and preaching not only throughout his usual area of Bedfordshire and Cambridgeshire but across Hertfordshire and Essex. He is thought to have spent some time at Bocking in Essex and to have made several visits to London where he made several friends. Shortly after *The Holy War* had been published, a group of fanatics had tried to kill King Charles and his brother James (heir to the throne) as they passed The Rye House, near Royston in Hertfordshire. They had been discovered and several of them were arrested and tried. To the horror of the Independent Church and probably many other people from Bedfordshire and elsewhere, Lord William Russell (of Woburn) was executed because he was wrongly suspected of involvement in the treasonable plot.

For some years Lord Russell had represented Bedfordshire in Parliament and had tried to shelter the Independents from the worst of the persecution. Following the 'Plot', there was a back-lash against both Roman Catholics and Independents.

Unlike Lord Russell, the Earl of Ailesbury encouraged this persecution and went out of his way to link independence of religious thought with politics, if not treason. In the January of 1685, he encouraged the county magistrates to put into execution, '... all such Laws as had been provided for the reducing all Dissenters to a thorow Conformity...'. However, within three weeks King Charles had died and his Roman Catholic brother was confirmed as King James II. During the religious and political upheavals that followed, the Bedford church were again persecuted by magistrates, church courts and by informers.

Although, like everyone else in his church, Bunyan was frustrated and distressed at his enforced silence and his inability to preach and teach openly, he made use of the time to keep on writing.

He and his friends continued to meet and preach in distant orchards and barns, moving around from place to place, always one stage ahead of the informers but he knew that any night the local constables could appear and take him back to prison.

A Deed of Gift

In prison he could continue to read, pray and write letters and pamphlets but what about his family. What would happen to them if he was imprisoned again? The older children were already leaving home. It is possible that the 'John Bunyan' recorded as living in Cranfield during 1671, (Hearth Tax) was John's eldest son. He lived in

Bedford in later years but may have left home when he first married. The second son, Thomas III, was either engaged or had just married; his daughter Elizabeth, had been married for several years and Sarah, the first of the children by his second marriage, was already engaged. It is possible that Thomas III and his new wife, Frances, were living with Elizabeth and that John wanted to make quite sure that her position was secure if anything should happen to him. He thought about it for some time and a few days before Christmas 1685, he drew up a deed of gift. He described himself as 'brazier' and wrote '... in consideration of the natural affection and love which I have and bear into my well-beloved wife, Elizabeth Bunyan, as also for divers other good causes and considerations me at this present especially moveing, have given and granted...'

Then he went on to describe his intentions that Elizabeth should have complete right to all his goods and chattels, ready money, household stuff and bedding, his clothes and his rings, such brass and pewter as they had managed to collect. Plus, in the Bunyan family's case something quite important for her future comfort – any debts owing to him. This could include money due from *The Pilgrim's Progress*. He asked four of his friends to witness the deed and then having decided not to show it to Elizabeth for the time being, hid it between some broken bricks in the chimney.

However this time he was lucky and managed to stay out of prison.

CHAPTER NINETEEN

The Last Years of Bunyan's Life

Even while *The Holy War* was being printed and circulated, Bunyan continued writing sermons and pamphlets, either concerning some theological point which was under discussion generally or on a subject he had been called to advise on, within his own 'parish'.

However, he could see that the more serious pieces that he wrote, would never reach a very wide readership. Thousands of people from all walks of life had read and hopefully benefitted from *The Pilgrim's Progress*; he must try and give these distant and unknown Christians some more help and guidance. Neither the cautionary tale of Mr Badman or the adventure story, wherein the devil attacked the town of Mansoul, had reached anything like the same readership.

Throughout the years, his pilgrim, Christian, had stayed beside him and no doubt he had used this theme on numerous occasions when talking to children or to simple people without a great understanding of moral theology. There were more situations that he would like to introduce and he couldn't escape from the occasional criticism, which is more common today, that Christian had abandoned his family to their fate when he set out on his journey to find salvation. Possibly, as with the original *The Pilgrim's Progress*, he wrote the second part over a number of years.

There are clues in several of his books which indicate how great an affection he had for children. They also suggest that not only his own children but possibly his grandchildren and the children of his friends, would watch out for him and greet him with pleasure. Many of the characters which Christian and then Christian's wife and children meet with on their journey may well have been tried out as bed-time stories.

The Pilgrim's Progress – Part II

It may also have been pressure from his publisher, Nathaniel Ponder
of London, which caused him in 1684 to hand over the manuscript of
The Pilgrim's Progress – Part II. So great was the demand that other
authors had attempted to take up the story.

In this book, Bunyan relates that he was dreaming in a wood; he
dreams of a man called 'Sagacity' whom he questions about the well-
being of Christian's family. After some conversation, Bunyan in his
dream, sees 'Christiana' sitting by her fireside, thinking of Christian;
his life, his example and the desperate pleas he made for her to join in
his search for salvation. The last thing Bunyan had made Christian do,
at the end of Part One, was to send a loving and encouraging message
to Christiana.

Sitting there, by her own fireside, she realises how foolish she has
been. The next day, while she is praying for advice, an angel visits her
and points out that she and the children could do a similar pilgrimage
of their own. She at once prepares herself and the five children for a
long journey and they are on their way.

Their route was much the same as that taken by Christian but with
great perception Bunyan realised that women would not fight against
some of the obstacles in the same way as men.

Also women were less likely to fall into The Slough of Despond and
were more likely to be given help with the problems that they came up
against.

Although, like most 17th-century books, its style is sometimes
difficult for a modern reader, contemporary readers could identify
with the dangers of the two ladies, Christiana and her friend Mercy
who decides to accompany her, as they walk along the lonely roads.
They would also smile with understanding when Christiana's children
picked up the windfall of forbidden fruit which fell from the devil's
apple trees, only to feel Christiana's panic when her son, Matthew
develops a terrible stomach ache and is doubled up in pain. Being an
allegory, the pills which the doctor uses to cure him are referred to as
'The Body and Blood of Christ'. As was the way with doctors, Bunyan
wrote that phrase in Latin but, in case his readers should think that he
really was a scholar after all, wrote 'The Latin I borrow'.

Christiana's journey is nothing like as severe as that of her husband;
the difficulties are not so great and the obstacles are not so menacing.
They take longer over their journey, resting along the way, and the

book has been criticized because the story line is not quite so tight and the spiritual message is not quite so clear. Maybe this is the writing of an older man who looks at the religious debates of his day with more experience and maturity.

Eventually Christiana and her family all reach the river which leads to Salvation but it is of interest that the children do not cross with their mother.

Book For Boys And Girls

The year in which this final part of *The Pilgrim's Progress* was published was the same year that the renewed persecution led him to make his deed of gift to Elizabeth. Although he did not know it, a series of events were about to take place which would eventually lead not only to his own freedom but gradually to complete freedom of worship.

The first major change was that King Charles II died and his Roman Catholic brother was crowned King James II. Bunyan was not prevented from preaching but during the unsettled period which followed the coronation he took the opportunity to publish two more pamphlets and to 'polish' and prepare for publication the many poems that he had previously written for children.

I have quoted several of these delightful poems in Chapter 3. They were published in 1686, entitled *A Book For Boys And Girls*. Although not widely read today, of all of the writing that he has left us these are the easiest to read, possibly the most enjoyable and give us the most insight into the nature of the young John Bunyan, the boy from Elstow village.

By this time, affairs at Court were already causing changes which rippled slowly out as far as Bedfordshire. Soon after James had been crowned, his illegitimate nephew, The Duke of Monmouth, had led the rebellion which ended with the Duke's execution, following the Battle of Sedgemoor. He was a Protestant who, willingly or not, was the figurehead at the centre of the anti-Roman Catholic party.

After Monmouth had been implicated in the Rye House plot, he had chosen to hide at Toddington Manor with the widowed Lady Wentworth and her daughter, Henrietta, so he was well known in parts of Bedfordshire. As the Wentworths had accompanied him into exile and had helped in a small way to finance the rebellion, Independents

The Old Baptist Chapel, Dunstable. An offshoot of the Kensworth meeting. D17

in Bedfordshire may have especially feared reprisals.

James's victory at Sedgemoor had scattered those who were violently against a Roman Catholic king. This made it possible for him to try out various schemes whereby he might be able to introduce one or two Roman Catholic friends into positions of authority. At first this caused a backlash which made things even more difficult for the Independent Church. Then, in apparent desperation, during 1687, James published a 'Declaration of Indulgence', which exempt both Roman Catholics and Nonconformists from all penal laws and tests. This was repeated the following year when he ordered that it should be read in all places of worship throughout the land.

The following months saw a situation where the prospective Members of Parliament were trying to persuade the Independents to support them back into government with promises of a declaration of freedom passed by an elected parliament.

Meanwhile James was sending round officials to try to use the new charter issued to Bedford Corporation by his brother, with the objective of putting Independents into numerous civil positions where they could give him support.

Bunyan may have been writing but he did not publish during this period. Intelligent man that he was, he could see through the invitations of both sides and was disgusted by them. It is possible that he himself was invited by one of James's officials to take on the position of magistrate. If he was, he certainly refused and advised his friends to do likewise.

Meanwhile, Edward Russell, nephew of the Duke of Bedford, was one of the men of several different political and religious persuasions who was in contact with the Dutch Prince of Orange. When the Prince and his fleet arrived at Torbay Harbour, they were joined by many English soldiers of all ranks. James fled to France and left England for some months without a King.

Parliament met and after some discussions invited the Prince of Orange and his wife, Anne, daughter of the ex-king, to be King and Queen of England. Before they were crowned they were asked to sign a 'Declaration of Rights' which included a clause that election of members of parliament should be free and that Parliament should be held frequently.

One of the first Acts which was passed was the 'Toleration Act', liberating Dissenters from penal statutes.

The Death of John Bunyan

However, Bunyan never knew about this act which removed the final risk of imprisonment from those who refused to attend their parish church.

He was in his sixtieth year but during the first half of 1688 he continued riding around the countryside, visiting the Independent Churches which he had helped to set up or which he had encouraged to keep going during the difficult years of persecution. Sometimes, he would ride great distances in response to an invitation to attend a meeting as guest speaker.

Despite all this travelling he kept in constant touch with the Bedford

Church and acted for them when discussions were necessary with other churches. He had never lost his gift of communication and was still called upon to counsel church members who had spiritual problems or who were tempted by the sins of the flesh.

When he heard that one of his Bedford friends was distressed because of an estrangement with a wayward son, he offered to ride to the young man's home in Reading to try and arrange a reconciliation. He was successful in his mission and set out one morning to visit his friend, John Strudwick, a grocer in Snowhill, London. Although it was August, he was caught in a rain storm and rode for many miles in soaking wet clothes. He managed to preach a sermon at the Petticoat Lane Meeting House on the following Sunday, but, not feeling well, he then stayed on in London. A day or two later he was persuaded to stay in bed; by this time, however, his fever was too great to respond to the treatments available and after many days of acute illness, he died on 31 August 1688, only a few weeks before the arrival of the future King William.

He was buried in the Dissenter's Cemetery at Bunhill Fields where his effigy can be seen to this day but his greatest memorial was *The Pilgrim's Progress*. His own 60-years' journey of hard work, emotional strain and spiritual anxiety, his concern for his much loved family, his imprisonment and, above all, his sheer dogged determination to reach the Celestial City, bears much resemblance to the pilgrimage undertaken by Christian. The only real difference is that in his later years his role included that of The Evangelist. In his lifetime he personally guided hundreds of his contempories through the wicket gate and onto the difficult road which leads via the obstacles of life to heaven.

Since his death, his writing, especially *The Pilgrim's Progress*, has helped many thousands of people, who have no knowledge or understanding of the type of problems that Bunyan had to wrestle with, but who found within his writing inspiration to start, and encouragement to continue with, a pilgrimage of their own.

The Bunyans of Elstow

The early years of the Elstow Parish Registers have long been missing but the chapman Thomas I (grandfather of John) had a son baptised Thomas II on 24 February 1603. An older son and daughter, Edward and Elizabeth, are mentioned in his will and their marriages are recorded – Edward married Rose Bentley (sister of John Bunyan's mother) on 31 August 1629 and Elizabeth, a local farmer called Thomas Watson, on 3 May 1618.

The death of their mother is not recorded but she may not have survived the birth of Thomas II. Left with a baby and two young children, Thomas I remarried on 18 November 1603 and in the next 11 years, his new wife, Elizabeth, (née Leighe), had four sons and three daughters of which only son John, baptised 16 October 1605 and daughters, Alice, baptised 12 April 1614, and Isobel, baptised 1 September 1616, survived the first few weeks of life.

Unfortunately, nothing more is known about these three children, none of whom are mentioned when their father made his will in 1641. Elizabeth Bunyan (née Leighe) died in April 1620 by which time Thomas I's first family had grown up and daughter Elizabeth had married. Edward was a bachelor of around 20 and Thomas II just under 17 was training to become a brazier, but Elizabeth's own children were much younger. John I was 14 and already at work but the two girls were only six and three-and-a-half. Their father, the chapman, was still not much over 40 and was no doubt often away from home so two months later he married again.

His third wife, Elizabeth (née Enwell) had no children of her own and by the time that she died, ten years later, the youngest step-child was 14. However, a new generation was coming along. The eldest son, Edward, was still a bachelor but Thomas II and his second wife, had a two-year-old boy, John I, and a one-year-old daughter.

A few months later, Thomas I married again, his fourth wife being the widow of 'Shepherd John Bidkin' who had died in October 1631 leaving to his widow his cottage in Elstow High Street. It was left to her unconditionally and she married Thomas Bunyan I 1 May 1632. On 27 August 1632 a deed was drawn up stating:

> I Anne Bonyon of Elstowe... wheras John Bidkin late of Elstow... Shephard my late Husband deceased did by his last will and Testament... give and bequeth unto me the said Anne Bonyon and my heires for ever all his Messuage and Tenement wherein I now dwell And Three Acres of Arable land therto belonging... in Considerac'on of the entyre love and affection which I have and beare unto my loving Husband Thomas Bonyon of. Elstow... Brasier for his better Maintenannce of living after the decease of me the said Anne Bonyon... And by this my present wrighting or deed doe ffreely Clearly and absolutly give Graunt enfeoffe and Confirme unto Thomas Bonyon my said Husband his heires and assignes for ever after the decease of me the said Anne Bonyon All that Messuage or Tenement with appurtenances Wherein Thomas Bonyon my said Husband and I doe now dwell....

Two years later they sold a piece of their joint holding in Quechssonne (Quicksand?) Meadow to Nicholas Waddope, mat maker, to join up with a piece that he already held. It is unlikely that it was true quicksand but it may well have been marshy and part of the area which is now drained and known as 'The Moor'. It could have been used as a reed-bed for thatchers and mat makers.

A reed bed behind Bromham Mill such as would have been owned or rented by a 17th century mat-maker. E7

A 'Bunyan' Cottage in the High Street, Elstow

The years went by and as they grew older, Thomas began to worry as to what would happen to Anne when he died, as she was still quite young. (She did not die until 1659). The village carpenter, George Eckles, wanted to sell his cottage which backed on to 'Pinfold Green' and was north of The Chequer Inn (long since gone), so Bunyan bought this sometime before 1636 and when he died in December 1641 Anne was independent. The building which is the present village post office, may be on the site.

In his will the old man left John and his other grandchildren, 6 pence (2½p) each. Anne who must have been younger than her husband, went on living in the village until her death. They were both

Elstow Post Office. Possibly on the site of the cottage owned by John Bunyan's grandfather. F9

buried in Elstow churchyard but the exact site is no longer known. Much less is recorded about members of the next generation, John's uncles and aunts. The marriages of Edward and Elizabeth have been already noted above but very little is known about his step uncles and aunts. His father, Thomas II, trained as a brazier and he married Anne Purney (or Pinney) on 10 January 1623 just before his twentieth birthday. There is no record of any children and four years later, in April 1627, she died. Less than six weeks later, Thomas II aged 24, married Margaret Bentley, an Elstow girl, who was just a few months younger than himself.

The author, John Bunyan, was born 18 months later and was baptised in Elstow church on 30 November 1628. His sister Margaret was baptised on 7 March 1630 and William on 21 October 1632. This was Margaret's last baby and the unusually small family stayed together in the cottage at Harrowden until the summer of 1644 when John's mother and sister died, in the June and July. Soon afterwards John joined the Parliamentary army.

When his wife, Anne (née Purney) died, Thomas II had waited less than six weeks before marrying Margaret Bentley. He no longer had young toddlers at home to need mothering but the death of both Margarets, within a few weeks of each other, caused a domestic crisis. John was preparing to go in the army, and meanwhile travelling the roads with his father. William, who was not yet 11 could not be expected to look after himself and do the work of the cottage and small-holding.

During the Civil War, Parish Registers were either not kept up at all, or their entries were unreliable, so the third marriage of John's father is not recorded. However, within a few weeks of the death of John's mother, probably a little while longer than between the death of Anne and his marriage to Margaret, Thomas II married another 'Anne'. The baptism of their son Charles is recorded at Elstow as 22 May 1645 followed by his burial, eight days later. A year or two later they had another son, baptised Thomas III, and two daughters Mary and Elizabeth.

It is possible that Thomas and Anne had moved into Grandad Bunyan's (Thomas I) cottage after his death, because by the time that the assessors made a visit for the Hearth Tax of 1671, there were no Bunyans living in Harrowden and Thomas was in a small cottage in Elstow. Thomas II died in February 1676 and his third wife Anne lived on until 1680.

When he made his will, during the previous May, he left John and his three younger children, a shilling each and the rest of his humble possessions to his widow.

Meanwhile, John Bunyan had returned from the army in 1647, to set up in business as a tinker. He married a young girl who is referred to as Mary because that was the name that they chose for their eldest daughter. Neither of them had any money or furniture and as John was apparently unwilling to intrude on his father's new family, they presumably rented a house or rooms in Elstow; maybe with his widowed grandmother? There was no forge and this may be one reason why he describes himself as 'tinker' as compared to his father, the 'brazier'. He made himself a travelling anvil and engraved it on one side 'J. BVNYAN' and on the other, '1647 HELSTOWE'. This can be seen in the Bunyan Museum in Bedford. It is said to weigh 60 lbs, so he must have had a pony or donkey and maybe a cart.

John and Mary had a daughter, who was baptised Mary at Elstow Church on 20 July 1650. She was born blind and concern about her must have added to John's misery when he was going through his religious crisis before he met John Gifford. He was certainly worried about her future when many years later, he knew he was in danger of transportation. The date of her death was not recorded but she died before John finally left prison.

A second girl, Elizabeth, was baptised at Elstow on 14 April 1654. She grew up, joined the congregation at her father's church and married a friend of his, Gilbert Ashley, the Goldington miller, in 1677.

Soon after her birth the family moved into Bedford and settled on the eastern edge of Bedford, in St Cuthbert's Street. Their baptisms, if they were baptised, were not entered in the Parish Register but two boys were born, John, maybe 1656 and Thomas, maybe 1658. Both these boys grew up, married and had families of their own.

The death of John's wife Mary may have been caused by the birth of Thomas, but we do not know as the burial was not recorded. However, like his itinerant father, a wife and mother was essential and John very quickly remarried. His new wife was called Elizabeth but we do not know her surname or the place of her birth. She was soon pregnant and the shock of John's imprisonment caused her to go into premature labour and lose her first baby.

She brought up John's first four children and then conceived a daughter of her own, while John was on parole from prison. This baby, probably born in 1668, was named Sarah and she grew up to marry

William Browne at St Cuthbert's Church on 19 December 1686.
Sarah was walking before her father came home from prison and they were able to lead a normal family life. Their last baby, Joseph, was baptised at St Cuthbert's Church on 16 November 1672 when Sarah was about four, step-sister Elizabeth was 18 and the two step-brothers a few years younger.

At this time John was busy writing and travelling over a very wide area, so the responsibility of rearing these two babies and at the same time, three teenagers, fell on Elizabeth.

Neither of Bunyan's two wives can have had a very easy life. The first, who we refer to as Mary, married him before he was 20, and had just returned from the army.

The picture that he draws of a young couple sitting at home, reading and discussing passages from her precious books suggests a happy, domestic start to their married life. However, even if in the interest of illustrating his spiritual message he exaggerated his wild behaviour, her life in Elstow must have been at times, quite unbearable. She had the dreadfully difficult job of looking after her blind toddler, going through her second pregnancy, trying to be a cheerful and caring mother to the two little girls, while she carried the burden of her husband's severe depression and spiritual turmoil. The move to a home of their own in Bedford and the tranquil period which followed her husband's baptism was cut short by her death. Including the two boys born in Bedford, she had had four babies in eight years. Surely her steadfast determination in keeping the family together while her husband worked his way through to stability, deserves recognition?

Elizabeth, on the other hand, married Bunyan when he was a mature man of over 30. Still very young herself, she took on his four small children, quickly conceived and nearly lost her own life when her first baby was born prematurely following the shock of his arrest. She is more widely known than Mary because of her spirited attempt to obtain a pardon for her husband, but following that brief spell of publicity, her story is once more disregarded. Even if she was only 30 when Joseph was born, it cannot have been easy, being 'mother' and at times, sole parent to such a mixed family.

There is no evidence of actual poverty, possibly the two older boys contributed to the housekeeping, but certainly there was no money to spare for luxuries.

As the years went by and John's first family began to make plans for leaving home, Elizabeth's life should have become a little easier but

once again the Independent ministers were in danger of imprisonment. Bunyan must have been very worried about the security of his
family.

By 1685, Thomas IV who a few years previously had caused his
family great anxiety (see below) was planning to marry and although
there is no definite evidence, it is possible that he may have brought his
wife into the family home. This would have meant yet another
generation of babies joining the household! On the other hand,
Elizabeth was planning to marry and move away from Bedford.

After a great deal of thought, just before Christmas 1685, Bunyan
wrote out a deed whereby he gave Elizabeth complete right to all his
property (see page 171). He asked some of his friends to witness the
deed and then carefully put it away behind some loose bricks until it
should be needed.

It seems possible that he did not worry Elizabeth about the new
danger that hung over them, or if he did show her the paper, that he
did not show her the hiding place. When he died in London, nearly
three years later she did not attempt to produce it* and with two of his
friends had to administer his estate as though the deed had never been
written. The resulting inventory valued his entire property at less than
£43! Elizabeth lived on for some years in what must have been difficult
financial circumstances.

Before Bunyan died he had left two or three more manuscripts with
the printers, which were published after his death. At home, there
were various short articles and sermons which he had prepared but not
yet delivered to his publishers. Elizabeth consulted a publisher and on
11 June 1690, an advertisement was published in a London paper,
Mercurius Reformatus, explaining that the widow of John Bunyan,
author of the well received *The Pilgrim's Progress* and other excellent
books, wanted to print ten manuscripts which he had left unpublished.
One of his London admirers, Charles Doe, saw this advertisement and
resolved to publish them as one volume. It took him nearly two years
but he succeeded at last. Doe also published notes that he had written
himself, about meetings that he had attended at which Bunyan had
preached and some details of these sermons.

When Elizabeth died in 1691, there was still one sermon kept back
by the family but eventually Doe persuaded them to let him publish it.
It appeared in 1698, under the title of *The Heavenly Footman*. The last

---

*It remained hidden until renovations in the 19th century.

book to be published was one of the most important, yet it did not appear until 1765. It included the extremely personal account of Elizabeth's attempts to persuade the Assize judges to release her husband right back in 1661. The history of the manuscript is unclear but as it is the only one of Bunyan's works to deal with personal details of his life it may be that the family were reluctant to share it with unknown and maybe unsympathetic strangers.

It is probable that Bunyan's great granddaughter, Hannah (see below) preserved the manuscript and she died in poverty, so none of the Bunyan family made money from his writing.

When John Brown was completing his biography of John Bunyan in the early 1880s, he attempted to trace any remaining descendents of John Bunyan. He started by separating the family of John's young step-brother, Thomas III born c.1647, from that of John's son, Thomas IV, born c.1658, the youngest of Margaret's four children. Step-brother, Thomas III, was welcomed into the 'Bunyan Meeting' by John himself in 1673, and twenty years later joined the new church at Southill. He married Elizabeth Sutton from Little Staughton and lived at Northill, where he was buried in 1695. At the time of the 1671 Hearth Tax, the Sutton family had a large house in Northill but there are no Bunyans listed. However, there is a 'Thomas Bunyan' living in nearby Maulden. His wife was buried at Northill on 11 November 1681 and her death was entered in the Church Book at Bedford. Their only known son had died two years earlier.

John II, John Bunyan's eldest son, trained as a brazier and although he settled in Bedford, did not join the Bedford Meeting until the 27 June 1693. He played an increasingly active part in the day-to-day running of the church and like his father before him, was sometimes chosen to help reform and strengthen their weaker friends. His father would have had great sympathy with Brother Butcher, who in 1700 had amongst other faults a weakness for 'light unbecoming actions' such as Stoolball and the Maypole.

John II leased a house from Bedford Corporation in the area of Mill Lane and Lurk Lane, from 1705 until his death in December 1728. There is no record of his son or daughter-in-law but in his will, he bequeathed his lease and the house that he owned in St Cuthbert's Street (perhaps the family house) to his granddaughter, Hannah, whom he had brought up from childhood and who had continued to live with him. This is the Hannah who died unmarried in 1770, bringing an end to one line of John Bunyan's ancestry.

Margaret's other son, Thomas IV, also failed to produce a male heir to carry on the family name. He trained as a tailor but when he was about 21, he and two other young men, one of whose fathers was a member of John Bunyan's Church, decided to try and help two other young men who were in Bedford gaol. These were not men who had been imprisoned for their religious beliefs but a thief and the son of a respectable stonemason who had been imprisoned for passing bad coins into the community, which were made by travelling counterfeiters. Maybe these three young men, one of whom was the stonemason's apprentice, felt that the imprisonment was unjust or unfair, anyway, they met together to discuss the possibility of helping their friends to escape. Either they were overheard or the apprentice got frightened and reported them. He later informed the justices that the other two had tried to persuade him to steal horses; had he done so, they intended going out onto the country roads and acting as highwaymen! He even suggested that Thomas Bunyan had admitted to him, that with some of the others, he had spent a whole night hiding behind a hedge near Putenhoe waiting to rob a lone rider, but that the only passers by had all been riding in groups for safety, and so their night had been wasted.

The apprentice proved to be a very unreliable witness and the accused were let off with a caution but Thomas's brother John and the tailor for whom he worked, had to stand as sureties for his good behaviour. Miss Bell* has pointed out that John Bunyan's book *The Life and Death of Mr Badman* came out later in the same year and that Mr Badman had caused his Godly parents great distress by trying to avoid the Sunday meetings of their church and that when obliged to go would either go to sleep or sit talking and distracting his friends. Mr Wiseman and Mr Attentive agreed that such behaviour was in no way the fault of the parents and that some children who came 'polluted with sin into the world . . .' could not be helped by the good example of their parents.

There is no evidence that Thomas IV ever did join his father's church either during John's lifetime or afterwards. His marriage has not been found among the Parish Registers but his son, Steven, was baptised at St Cuthbert's Church on 14 November 1689. The baby's death is not recorded but he died soon after his birth and his mother, 'Frances', was buried at St Cuthbert's Church on 4 June, 1689.

*Miss P. Bell B.A., *John Bunyan and Bedfordshire* – see bibliography.

Thomas then married again, a lady called Katherine and a daughter, Elizabeth, was baptised at St Cuthbert's Church on 29 January 1693. (There is an illegible burial entry for 1711 which may be the young Elizabeth). Another baby boy was born in December 1696 and having decided to name him after Thomas's dead son, Steven, his parents arranged for him to be baptised on Christmas Day. In between the two later baptisms at St Cuthbert's Church, a 'Katherine Bunyan' became a member of what would become the 'Bunyan Meeting'.

Brown could not trace any further members of this line of the Bunyan family except the possibility of a Sarah Bunyan, who married John Millard at St Paul's Church in 1767 and an Ann Bunyan, who married Samuel Slinn at St Mary's Church in 1768, being the granddaughter of Thomas IV.

No surviving records have been found concerning Mary's blind daughter, Mary II but it is assumed that she died before her father. Mary's daughter Elizabeth, married Gilbert Ashley at Goldington Church, on 16 April 1677. He was a member of her father's church and when licences were first issued to the Independent Church, in 1672, his house at Goldington was one of the houses licensed for meetings.

There are no Ashleys recorded at Goldington when the Hearth Tax assessors visited in 1671 and no children have been discovered within the pages of the Parish Registers.

So no descendants have been traced from Mary's three surviving children. Of Elizabeth's children, Joseph, who was born in 1672, after his father had at last become a free man, had the benefit of his presence at home. On his marriage, in December 1694, to Mary Charnock, he appears to have moved into the centre of the town and lived in the Parish of St Paul's, and their first son, 'Chernock' was baptised at St Paul's Church on 6 October 1695. A daughter, Ann, was baptised 12 months later but she died within a month.

No further references to this branch of the family have been found but tradition links Joseph with the Bunyan families of Nottinghamshire and Lincolnshire. The Rev John Brown, Bunyan's biographer, was shown a family tree which was said to demonstrate the link between the Bunyans of Bedfordshire and those further north, but after extensive research, he was not convinced. It is, however, possible that modern genealogists would find that there are now documents available which would be able to prove the link.

Bunyan's youngest girl, Sarah, was born just before her father was released from prison and her marriage to William Browne is recorded in the Parish Register of St Cuthbert's Church, on 19 December 1686, nearly two years before her father's death. In 1671 the Browne's house was of a similar size to the Bunyan's and listed next to them.

John Brown could not find any records concerning Sarah's children but her granddaughter, Frances, who was born in 1722, later married Charles Bithrey, a comfortably off farmer who lived at the Manor Farm, called 'Fishers' at Carlton. She lived on until 1803 and Brown was able to talk to people who remembered this highly respected old lady. She was known in the village as 'Madam Bithrey' and after her husband's death, gave all the children a loaf of bread on the anniversary of his birthday. Unlike many of Bunyan's other descendants she remained loyal to the nonconformist tradition. She regularly attended the meeting at Carlton and helped to support the minister, the Rev. Charles Vorley. She had no children of her own and her nephew's children inherited much of her estate. The descendants of these 'Browne' boys, who lived at Carlton, Bedford and St Albans, could probably trace their ancestry back to Madam Bithrey's father and so to John Bunyan.

Some of her personal possessions, including a small cabinet which had been passed down through the Bunyan family, probably from John himself, she bequeathed to Mr Vorley the minister. Together with several other items of Bunyan's personal possessions, this can be seen at the Bunyan Museum, Bedford.

Elstow

'Reader, have you ever been to Elstow – THE Elstow that is situated in the county of Bedford? If not – go now. Are you a romantic temperament? then go and be inspired by its ruins, ivy, lovers' walks, and stiles . . .'.

So wrote James Wyatt in 1845*, and in 1988, I am quite in agreement with him; if only it wasn't for the incessant traffic! But don't be put off, do go, go early on a Sunday morning and wander up and down the High Street. The houses on the eastern side are much as John Bunyan knew them. What was a barn and what were craftsmen's workshops and at least one of the inns are all now private houses, but two of the inns are still in business and, of course, the church, the bell tower and the Moot Hall are all carefully preserved.

Medieval Elstow

The success of Elstow as a medieval village was originally due to the Benedictine Abbey of St Mary, although there was a community living here from Saxon times.

William I gave it to his niece Judith along with several other villages around Bedford and arranged for Judith to marry the only wealthy Englishman in the area who had agreed to support him. This was Waltheof, Earl of Huntingdon, who remained loyal for nearly three years but then joined the rebellion at York. He was forgiven this lapse but when a few years later he joined another rebellion he was imprisoned, and in 1076 he was executed.

Judith was left a widow and she founded the nunnery. One version

Elstow; its Maid of Honour, and its Pilgrim.

of the story is that she informed on her husband and this was her penance; another version is that she founded it in the sorrow of her widowhood. It was a wealthy and aristocratic house and early in the 12th century Henry I gave them a licence to hold a fair each year on the second to the fifth of May, to which merchants came from London and from miles around. There was a market cross on the green and rows of stalls selling foods, dairy products, cloth, wool, leather, pottery and many other things. There were smiths working with iron, steel and bronze, and no doubt there were booths with many forms of entertainment. At some date an area was fenced off for sales of sheep and cattle. The nuns had a rent from every stall or booth, even carts pulled up on the green had to pay 3d (1¼p); they also took a toll of all business done during the fair.

Being such a rich nunnery they attracted wealthy novices who may not always have had the correct vocation. After some years not all of them were wearing the obligatory black robes; some ladies were allowed to wear their own clothes. The idea of a communal dormitory, and refectory, where those eating were silent while one sister read from the Bible, was abandoned in favour of a series of 'houses' where groups of friends lived together as in families. Nevertheless the house survived and did not surrender to Henry VIII until August 1539 when there was an Abbess with 23 nuns. The nuns had owned not only Elstow village, farms and mill but also churches, villages and agricultural estates round about. They had needed people to administer all of these and this staff had needed shops and tradesmen, so a small town grew up around three sides of the green.

By the time that the young John Bunyan was old enough to toddle across the village green, the nunnery had mainly disappeared, but it was not forgotten. The people of Elstow had for centuries used a nave of the Abbey Church for their services and so after 1539, when the destruction was taking place, the east end was blocked off and the present St Helena's saved as a parish church.

On the floor was (and still is) a brass, depicting an abbess in her robes. This is Elizabeth Hervey who was abbess from 1501 to 1524. Henry VIII sold the nunnery and its land to Elizabeth's grand-nephew, Edmund Hervey. It passed from one member of the family to another until it was bought by a distant member of the same family, Thomas Hillersden. He set builders to work converting the western range of buildings and adding many new rooms to form The Hillersden Mansion.

The Abbey Church of St Mary and St Helena, the free standing bell tower and the remains of the Hillersden Mansion, Elstow. F9

This was not finished when he made his will in 1632 but he arranged for money to be made available so that it could be completed. The young John Bunyan and other village children must have looked forward to watching the stonemasons and carpenters at work.

John Bunyan's Elstow

Being on the main road only about two miles south of Bedford and holding regular fairs, the Elstow which John Bunyan knew was still a prosperous and active village.

Sheep, which were sold at the fairs, were an important part of the village economy. The cottage which John Bunyan's grandfather bought (possibly on the site of the village shop) backed on to Pinfold Green. His fourth wife, was the widow of the village shepherd who had not only owned his own cottage but also several acres of land.

Back in the 16th century, a wealthy farmer, William Curtes, left 40 ewes which the church-wardens were to rent out to one of the villagers and the income was to be used to help support the poor.

Despite the main road it was a very rural community; the lanes leading out to the common fields having names like Lambs Lane and Spinney Lane. Most of the men worked on the land or in other village crafts such as blacksmiths, wheelwrights, hurdle-makers, carpenters and mat makers.

Other men like those of the Bunyan family were local itinerant workers (chapmen and braziers) who walked around other villages, isolated hamlets and farms. There was at least one baker and probably another shop or two, a shoemaker, weaver and tailor. Being on the main road there may well have been a saddler and probably a carrier.

Most roadside villages which had plenty of inns to attract travellers, built up a second source of income, the work being done by wives and widows. In Elstow, several ladies were brewing a little beer and may have been preparing and selling food to travellers. Although there were so many inns it is possible that one of the roadside farmers may have been selling hay, oats and other supplies for horses.

The mats which were made from the local reed beds would have been sold by itinerant salesmen and in the market but no doubt special decorated mats, baskets and other fancy goods would have been sold to travellers either from a roadside workroom or in the inns. We know that the Fenn family of Bedford were hat makers and one or two Elstow families could have been making them and selling them to travellers.

The Inns of Elstow

Today, the Swan and the Red Lion stand on either side of the road welcoming travellers as they have done since well before the 17th century. The Chequers, which stood on the corner next to Thomas Bunyan's cottage has long since gone, as has the Catherine Wheel which, in the 17th century, also stood alongside the village green.

It was the responsibility of all religious houses to provide accommodation for travellers and many of these 'hostels' gradually became inns. Also as more and more travellers passed along the roads, the Prioress licensed the building of other inns. In the days of Elstow nunnery, the Green was lined with inns: the above-mentioned Chequers, the present Swan Inn then known as the Star and the Saracens which may have become The Catherine Wheel of Bunyan's day.

The Red Lion at Elstow. F9

On the other side of the road, the Red Lion was in business before 1600. The Newold family owned this inn from 1631 well into the next century. When John Newold made his will in February 1640 he was obviously a rich man. He left his wife, Mary, and eldest son, John, not only his house and land but also the remainder of his estate after bequeathing £30 each to his other son, William, and to his daughter, Maria.

Nearby is an archway which now leads through into the gardens and yards of the nearby houses. This may have been built as part of The Cock Inn which was on the opposite side of the road from the nunnery.

The Archway between houses in Elstow High Street, possibly once connected with the Cock Inn. F9

The Village Community

The day-to-day running of the village would have been the responsibility of the Manor Court. The steward who managed Hillersden House, or else his representative, would have been in charge and a committee of the more prosperous householders would have formed an informal jury. Matters decided by the court would be entered on the manor court rolls and at a later date arguments could be settled by referring back to an earlier judgement.

The interests of the lord of the manor were protected as anyone who wanted to cut a tree or alter their house, change their tenancy, or change the use of their buildings, would come to the court and formally ask permission and after due discussion probably get permission as long as the 'lord' was compensated with the customary 'fine'.

In the days when the 'open fields' were shared by many different people it was essential that there should be strict rules to protect the crops and anyone who allowed a beast to stray, or a ditch to overflow, would be 'summoned' to the court. Also, as grazing was also shared, each man's rights were strictly controlled and if anyone over-stocked or put their sheep out on to the grass before it was ready, they also were fined.

The lanes, especially the main one leading through to Harrowden, must be maintained for the good of all and carters who continually dropped mud or manure would be fined. In addition, both the lanes and the main road leading through the village would also have to be maintained by the village people. Each Easter at the annual church meeting two men would have been chosen to collect money from each householder and arrange a rota of men to do the actual labouring required.

No doubt there was at least one 'good wife' or experienced lady who would have helped the villagers in and out of this world and the richer people might have been able to consult the doctor in Bedford. Most families, however, would have relied on their own resources or help from their neighbours in times of trouble.

Because of the nearby county town, the constant activity at the inns and the excitement caused by the fairs, the people of Elstow, if they had the money to spend, would not have been restricted in their choice of food, clothes or of any other bought goods. Many of them must have had family or friends who either lived or worked in Bedford.

The Moot Hall

This is a traditional Bedfordshire market house and was built in the days of the nunnery and the timber frame is original although the walls would have been in-filled with wattle-and-daub.

It was built with four bays, three of which were let out in the form of six small shops and the fourth bay contained a ladder (later replaced by a staircase) which lead to the upper floor. By the time that John Bunyan knew the building a fifth bay had been added and the great brick chimney which made it possible to install fireplaces on both floors. This part may have been used as a 'caretaker's cottage' and much of the spare space would have been used for storing stalls, ropes and other things used at the market. Upstairs was the area reserved for whichever of Hillersden's staff were responsible for organising the fair

The Moot Hall, Elstow. F9

Pulpit from Elstow Church –
now in The Moot Hall. F9

and collecting rents, supervising the running of the fair, the quality of goods and checked that no one exceeded the fixed price for such goods as bread and beer.

There was always trouble at these sort of gatherings and any offender who was caught stealing, selling stolen goods, or picking pockets was taken straight upstairs and having been judged by an impromptu court was given a small fine on the spot or transferred to Bedford prison to await the next meeting of the local magistrates.

This same room may have been used to house the manor court and other public meetings. For a long time the Moot Hall was a focal point for the village, a small income being made by letting it out to such people as the landlord of the Red Lion who used it for storage. The Elstow Baptists used it at one time as a meeting house and the church held their first day school in the building.

Gradually it fell into disrepair. The large fairs came to a close towards the end of the 19th century and the sale of cattle ceased during the 1914–1918 war. It was no longer needed as a church or as a school and for some years it stood empty.

In 1951, Bedfordshire County Council restored the building as their main contribution to the Festival of Britain. Both the hall and the village green were given to the Council by County Alderman, Major Simon Whitbread DL, JP, and it was opened to the public on 31 May 1951.

It now houses an excellent exhibition of 17th-century furniture laid out as room settings and such items as the pulpit from which John Bunyan used to preach. It is regularly open to the public for a very low charge.

Places to Visit in
Bunyan's Bedfordshire Today

Although at first glance, Bedfordshire would appear to have changed out of all recognition since the days that John Bunyan walked its roads and lanes and visited its market towns, if one has the time to pick up a town trail from the Tourist Information Centre or ask the advice of the museum or library staff of the various towns within the county, you will find many medieval buildings hidden behind Georgian or Victorian facades. Look inside the shops and pubs which line the main roads and you stand a good chance of finding an exposed timber frame or a stone fireplace which has stood there since the 17th century or before.

Once out in the countryside you can stand in the centre of many Bedfordshire villages and know that the houses round about have actually witnessed the events relayed in this book.

Many of the pictures illustrate interesting things to be seen by anyone driving along the county's roads, but in some cases it will be necessary to visit buildings or gardens, on the days when they are open to the public.

Fortunately, Elstow village is exceptionally well preserved. Many of the houses in the High Street stood there when John Bunyan went to school. The date which can be seen on some of the houses, records the year that Samuel Whitbread had them repaired. He bought the estate in 1792.

In the 1970s the Whitbread Trust passed these buildings to North Bedfordshire Borough Council. As part of their celebrations for Queen Elizabeth's Silver Jubilee in 1977, the Council had the row repaired and carefully restored.

Cottages in Hockliffe – in the 17th century the Star Inn.   D16

Buildings in the Care
of Bedfordshire Leisure Services

Moot Hall, Elstow

One-and-a-half miles south of Bedford in Elstow village, just off the A6. Formerly a 16th-century medieval market hall. Marking of original shop units can still be seen on the ground floor. Parts of the original timber framing are clearly visible. Carefully restored in 1951 the building is now open to the public as a museum housing a collection of furniture and artifacts of the 17th century period, an exhibition of translations of Bunyan's *The Pilgrim's Progress*; a room depicting life in the time of John Bunyan and sales area specialising in books relating to Bunyan and other local history topics. It stands on the pleasant village green where Bunyan played tip-cat and other games.

The Moot Hall and Elstow Green were given to Bedfordshire County Council by County Alderman, Major Simon Whitbread and the council restored it as their main contribution to the Festival of Britain.

Telephone: (01234) 228330 for opening times and other information.

Bromham Mill.   E7

Bromham Watermill

2 miles west of Bedford, just off the A428 Bromham bypass, by Bromham Bridge. Mentioned as mill site in Domesday Book. Earliest parts of present mill date from 1695 with later parts added in the 1850s. Carefully restored, the ground and first floors are now open to the public and house restored and working water-wheel and associated machinery; exhibition of old agricultural and milling machinery; static exhibitions on natural and local history; history of milling and of waterways and natural history room, of particular interest to children.

There is also a small intimate art and sculpture gallery on the first floor with changing exhibitions each month. The Great Ouse runs by the mill, alongside which is an attractive picnic site with tables and benches.

Telephone: (01234) 228330 for opening times and other information.

Swiss Garden, Old Warden

In the village of Old Warden, next to the Shuttleworth Collection of old aircraft. Formerly owned by the Ongley family. Early 19th-century romantic landscaped garden and ornamental buildings, including thatched summer-house, chapel and kiosk; artifacts; a wide variety of trees – some rare; ponds; interesting walks and vistas; tranquil lakeside picnic area with tables and benches.

Telephone: (01234) 228330 for opening times and other information.

Churches

The Abbey Church of St Mary and St Helena, Elstow

Where John Bunyan worshipped as a young man; and the freestanding tower where he rang the bells stands alongside. Near the Moot Hall in the centre of Elstow.

Admission: Any reasonable time.

St John's Church

Where John Gifford helped the young John Bunyan, still stands as a Parish Church on the south side of Bedford, but the rectory is now the local headquarters of the St John's Ambulance.

Details from the Tourist Information Office, Bedford. Telephone: (01234) 215226.

Stained glass window at the Bunyan Meeting Free Church, Bedford.

The Bunyan Meeting Free Church, Bedford, and Bunyan Museum

Bunyan Meeting is the oldest non-conformist church in Bedford and is referred to in a recent European guide as one of the most historic Independent Churches in the world.

The church was founded in 1650 and moved to its present site in 1672 when John Bunyan and others purchased a barn and part of an orchard in Mill Street. The first purpose-built church was erected in 1707, this was replaced by the present building in 1850. Further buildings were added at the rear in 1868 and 1892.

Significant features include: the Communion Table which is part of the original Table used for the celebration of Communion in the barn; the stained glass windows depicting scenes from Bunyan's life and *The Pilgrim's Progress* were all installed this century; the celebrated bronze entrance doors with their illustrative panels were the gift of Hastings, 9th Duke of Bedford in 1876.

Adjoining the church is the Bunyan Museum which houses Bunyan memorabilia, and among other items, over 160 editions of *The Pilgrim's Progress* in many different languages.

The Museum is open during the summer months when it welcomes visitors from all over the world.

Details from the Tourist Information Office, Bedford. Telephone: (01234) 215226.

★ ★ ★

Several of the houses once lived in by the 17th-century landowners are still standing and information about occasional opening dates for the houses or the gardens can be obtained from Tourist Information Centres throughout Bedfordshire.

Houses in the Care of English Heritage Regularly Open To The Public

Bushmead Priory

On an unclassified road near Colmworth, 2 miles east of the B660. Was once the medieval refectory of an Augustinian priory, with rare timber-frame roof of crown post construction. Contains wall paintings and interesting stained glass. In the 17th century it was the home of the Gery family.

Telephone: (01234) 215226 for opening times and other information.

Wrest Park House and Gardens

Three-quarters of a mile east of Silsoe off the A6.
The formal gardens were laid out for the Duke of Kent in the early 18th century, later partly remodelled by Capability Brown and others. The principal rooms on the ground floor of the house were built 1834–39 in the French style and are open to the public. In the 17th century, this house was owned by the Grey family; a descendant of whom became the Duke of Kent.

Telephone: (01234) 215226 for opening times and other information.

The Grey Family Mausoleum

At nearby Flitton; it is attached to the church on an unclassified road one-and-a-half-miles west of the A6 at Silsoe. It contains a magnificent collection of monuments including some of the 17th century.

Admission: Any reasonable time.

Houghton House

One mile north-east of Ampthill off A418, 8 miles south of Bedford. This is the remains of an early 17th century mansion built for Mary, Countess of Pembroke and with work attributed to Inigo Jones. During the life of John Bunyan it was the home of the Bruce family who became the Earls of Ailesbury.

As a local brazier was known to visit this house, it has been suggested that this was the 'House Beautiful' of Bunyan's *The Pilgrim's Progress*.

Admission: Any reasonable time.

Ruins of Lord Bruce's House at Ampthill (Houghton House). E/F12

Private Houses Regularly Open to the Public

Woburn Abbey

Home of the Marquess of Tavistock, is usually open weekends January to March and daily from the end of March to towards the end of October.

Woburn village is situated on the A418, almost midway (four/five miles) between the M1 (exit 13) and the A5 (turn at Hockliffe) and is 13 miles south west of Bedford. The Abbey is one-and-a-half miles from the village.

The Abbey contains an impressive and important private collection of paintings, furniture, porcelain and silver, the tour covering three floors, including the Crypt. There is also a 40-shop Antiques Centre, informal gardens, and a pottery, and nearby is the Woburn Wild Animal Kingdom, Britain's largest drive-through safari and leisure park.

Telephone: (01525) 290666 for further details.

Chicksands Priory

What is now RAF Chicksands is Ministry of Defence property. It is approximately seven miles south of Bedford, off the A600. During the life of Bunyan this was the home of the Osborne family and it is here, that Dorothy Osborne wrote her letters to William Temple.

It is presently open on the 1st and 3rd Sunday afternoon between April and October when tours are organised by The Friends of Chicksands Priory.

Telephone: (01234) 824195 for further information.

There are many books, pamphlets and maps available at Tourist Information Offices throughout the county which will help you discover 'Bunyan's Bedfordshire'.

A Trip Round
Bunyan's Bedfordshire Today

November 12th 1995 is the 335th anniversary of the arrest of John Bunyan as he began his meeting, at Lower Samsell Farm, Harlington. During those 300 plus years there have been many changes in Bedfordshire but nevertheless there are still features left which Bunyan would recognise today.

Unfortunately, the cottage where he was born, at 'Bunyan's End', in the fields between Elstow village and the outlying hamlet of **Harrowden**, has long since gone. A commemorative stone marks the spot and a footpath crosses the low lying, once marshy, fields (Slough of Despond?) along which he used, reluctantly, to walk to church and probably to school.

Elstow

If in 1995 he walked once more beside the ditches, which drain the marshy ground, he would be amazed to come out on to a well made **High Street** with pavements, but would recognise many of the houses.

In 1792, Samuel Whitbread, the famous brewer and social reformer, bought the village and had all the cottages so well repaired that when in the 1970s the Whitbread Trust passed these buildings to North Bedfordshire Borough Council, they were able to successfully restore them, and to leave the street scene, apart from its present cleanliness(!), as it was in the 17th century. Also thanks to the care of the Whitbread family the Manor Court Rolls and many property deeds have survived, adding to our knowledge of both the Bunyan family and Elstow.

The deeds of both inns, the Swan and the Red Lion, go back to John Bunyan's childhood. We do not know in which cottage the 'loose and ungodly wretch' lived, who referred to Bunyan as '. . . the ungodliest fellow, for swearing that she ever heard in her life'. We are however fairly certain which cottage Thomas Bunyan bought as a marriage settlement for his third wife, Anne Bidkin. The deeds of the present post office – general stores mention both Thomas Bunyan and the correct location. When John married for the first time and set up house without '. . . having so much household stuff as a dish or spoon betwixt us . . .' he *may* have lived at this house, in the High Street, when he first returned from the Civil War. The cottage where they settled, and where their daughters Mary and Elizabeth were born, has gone. A plaque marks the site, in the car park of the St. Helena Restaurant.

The Moot (village) Hall which John knew well, was again preserved by the Whitbread family. This was given to Bedfordshire County Council, who restored it and opened it to the public. It houses a collection of antique furniture of the 17th century, a room setting of a typical farmhouse living room and many things associated with John Bunyan.

Behind the hall is the well cared for **Village Green**, where John and his friends played Tip-Cat and other noisy games. Behind that is the extremely beautiful **Church of St. Mary and St. Helena**. This is where John, his brother, sister and his own two daughters were baptised and where Sunday after Sunday he sat listening to the Rev. Christopher Hall and where he heard what he took as a personal reprimand on the wickedness of playing games on Sunday. Christopher Hall's pulpit is on display in the Moot Hall but the baptismal font is still in use in the church.

On one side of the church, overlooking the Green, is the famous **Bell Tower**, still in use today. Here, because of the growing opinion that bell ringing on the Sabbath was wrong, he struggled to subdue his love of ringing. With the clouds behind it, on a windy day, the tower does indeed appear to sway!

On the other side, facing the private paddock, under which are the foundations of a nunnery, are the remains of the **Hillersden Mansion** which was being built during John Bunyan's childhood.

BEDFORD, just up the road from Elstow, lies on either side of the **River Ouse** and a plaque marks the place of John's adult baptism.

South of the river, **St. John's** is still an active parish church but **The Rectory** where John Gifford, friend, counsellor and spiritual adviser to the distraught young Bunyan lived, is now the headquarters of the St. John's Ambulance Brigade.

North of the river, St. Cuthbert's, where John's sons are thought to have been baptised, and where his daughter Sarah was married, is still standing but the nearby house to which the growing family moved has gone. However, on the exact site in Mill Street, where, in 1672, Bunyan and his friends bought a barn and part of an orchard, stands the **Bunyan Meeting Free Church and Museum**. The present building was put up in 1850, with additions in 1868 and 1892. Not only does the church contain the stained glass window, of Bunyan in prison, made famous by Terry Waite but of even more importance is the communion table which is part of the original table, used for the celebration of communion by John Bunyan and his friends.

Bedford Borough Council have produced a **pictorial leaflet/trail** for those wanting to explore John Bunyan's Bedford and Elstow and the staff at the **Tourist Information Centre**, in St. Paul's Square, are there to help.

Harlington

During the 1980s the famous **Bunyan Oak**, at Lower Samsell Farm, where traditionally John Bunyan was arrested, began to drop its branches. As part of the commemorative events, marking the tercentenary of the 300th anniversary of Bunyan's death, in 1988, internationally acclaimed botanist, Dr David Bellamy, planted a new young tree which now stands beside its historic brother.

Several of the timber-framed and thatched cottages which Bunyan passed, as he walked or rode from Samsell Farm to Harlington Manor House, still stand today as does the beautiful and historic **Church of St. Mary**. In 1660 the vicar was the Rev. Dr Lindall, father-in-law of the magistrate, Francis Wingate J.P. and who encouraged Wingate to order the arrest. Today Bunyan is very much respected by the vicar and his congregation. They are proud of their stained glass 'Pilgrim' window and of their new communion table, carved by a local carpenter, from one of the fallen branches of 'Bunyan's oak'.

The Manor House, to which the constable took Bunyan to await Wingate's arrival, still stands today and is lovingly cared for by its present owner. This is a private house, not open to the public, but part of the grounds have been walled off and there is a warm welcome at the newly opened **Manor Restaurant**.

Many of the Bedfordshire villages have connections with John Bunyan or are thought to have been in his mind as he sat in Bedford prison writing *The Pilgrim's Progress*. A drive around these villages, with their churches, pubs, village greens and duck ponds is an extra pleasure to round off a visit to Bunyan's Bedfordshire.

APPENDIX V

Searching for Sites in The Pilgrim's Progress – A Bedfordshire Pastime

In 1901, the Vicar of Elstow, A. J. Foster, published 'Bunyan's Country. Studies in the Bedfordshire Topography of "The Pilgrim's Progress".' Since then it has become a Bedfordshire pastime to try and link real places with the sites described in Bunyan's famous book.

John Bunyan was son and grandson of men whose work took them out into the Bedfordshire countryside. It therefore seems likely that he would have accompanied them as a boy and would have thought back on those formative childhood journies, when he was a man imprisoned in Bedford gaol.

The Slough of Despond

'Now I saw in my dream . . . they drew near to a very miry Slough . . .
The name of the Slough was Despond.'

Wet marshy stretches of path or road were common in 17th century Bedfordshire and many suggestions have been offered for Bunyan's Slough. My own choice is *the path which led from his home, at Bunyan's End, to Elstow Church*, where he probably went reluctantly to school. It was, and in part still is, a marshy piece of ground.

Mount Sinai

Christian was distracted off the route, advised by Evangelist, and found his road blocked by a hill, from which occasionally came flames.

'. . . it seemed so high, and also that side of it that was next the wayside, did hang so much over, that Christian was afraid to venture further, lest the Hill should fall on his head.'

Risinghoe Castle, near Goldington, is a very high motte on which a medieval castle once stood. By the 17th century all that was left was an exceptionally steep grass mound near to a place where the farmer sometimes made bricks. From time to time flames may well have escaped from the kiln.

The House of the Interpreter

'Then he went on till he came at the House of the Interpreter . . .'

In his spiritual autobiography Bunyan tells us that in one of his worst periods of confusion, he sat '. . . under the ministry of holy Mr Gifford, whose doctrine, by God's grace, was much for my stability'. *Gifford's Church of St. John, Bedford*, is still a busy parish church. His *rectory* is today the county centre for the St. John's Ambulance Brigade. Strengthened by the encouragement that he received from the Interpreter, Christian set out to find the cross of redemption.

The Cross and the Sepulchre

'So I saw in my dream, that just as Christian came up with the Cross, his burden loosed from off his shoulders, and fell from off his back; and began to tumble, . . . till it came to the mouth of the sepulchre, where it fell in and I saw it no more.'

The Independent 'church' at Stevington enjoyed help and co-operation from John Gifford and the congregation at St. John's. *The Medieval Cross in the centre of Stevington* still stands today and one road runs down hill, past the church of St. Mary the Virgin, to a *spring of fresh water, which bubbles out through a man-made arch,* below the churchyard wall. The cross isn't cruciform, the details are not exact, but the brave Stevington Independents, whose belief carried them through the years of persecution, may have helped to inspire the story of the cross and the burden tumbling down and disappearing into the mouth of the Sepulchre.

The Hill of Difficulty

He approached this hill with two companions; but put off by its steepness, they left him and found a way round.

If this hill was represented by *Hazlewood Hill, north of Ampthill,* both alternative paths would have been strictly private and anyone foolish enough to trespass would have risked mutilation by mantraps. One crossed the wooded hunting park of Ampthill and the other the uneven, rough-pastured park of Houghton House.

The Lions

Half-way up the hill Christian met 'Mistrust' and 'Timourous', hurrying back down, frightened by lions. Just as some country houses were guarded by fierce, chained dogs, to keep visitors from straying off the drive, so Christian's lions also turned out to be chained. He continued on his way.

The Palace Beautiful

'. . . he lift up his eyes, and behold there was a very stately palace before him, the name whereof was Beautiful, . . .'

Today *the ruins of Houghton House, Ampthill,* stand near the brow of Hazlewood Hill; they are in the care of English Heritage. The house was less than fifteen years old when John Bunyan was born and was the most exciting and imaginative building in this part of England. It was the home of the Bruce family, Earls of Ailsbury; they are known to have employed all manner of craftsmen and salesmen. Bunyan would have seen it, from a distance, perched on its hill and may have visited it. From prison it could have stuck in his memory as a 'beautiful palace'.

The Delectable Mountains

From the palace his hostesses pointed out the view to the south.

'. . . at a great distance he saw a most pleasant mountainous country, . . . , with springs and fountains . . .'

The chalk hills, which form a backcloth to the beautiful countryside of South and Mid Bedfordshire, could be imagined as suggesting this imagery. Also, *the Barton Hills are famous for their springs,* which tumble down the hillside.

The Valley of Humiliation

He was warned that it wasn't easy to descend into this valley. If his road ran south into Ampthill it is still steep and overshadowed by trees today. Although this pleasant market town is noted for its Georgian buildings, others are much older than they appear. Whether Bunyan had cause to associate Ampthill with humiliation we do not know, but the rector and several of his congregation were strict Anglicans and ardent Royalists.

Somewhere in the Valley of Humiliation Christian met and conquered Apollyon before heading into another fearful valley.

The Valley of the Shadow of Death

He knew that the valley was as dark as pitch and that the narrow road had a quagmire on one side and a deep pit on the other. He was told there would be:

'. . . hobgoblins, satyrs, and dragons, . . . howling and yelling, as of a people under unutterable misery.'

The road from Ampthill into Millbrook climbs sharply. The manorial rabbit warren, with its deep holes, traps, gins and nets, later referred to by Bunyan, used to be on the left of the road, and *a deep wooded gorge can still be seen.*

The Church of St. Michael and All Angels is perched even higher on the hill; its attractive churchyard, high on the very edge of the Greensand Ridge, overlooks the valley-clay and the church of Marston Morteyne. The 17th century brickworks, with smoke and flames escaping from the kilns and with the sack-clothed, bare-footed workers might well have inspired some of Christian's terrifying encounters.

As a boy Bunyan would have known the story of the three 'Devil's Jump Stones' – one of which still stands in a field near Marston. The devil is said to have stolen the bell tower of St. Mary's Church, dropped it, where it stands, separated from the main church building, and made three great leaps, marked by the stones. As a man he would never have felt safe in Millbrook or Marston, where the church ministers and some of their congregations had High Church and Royalist sympathies.

No sooner was Christian out of the valley than, having caught up with Faithful, they were both facing an entirely different danger. .

Vanity Fair

They came to a town which was already in a hubbub. Their unfamiliar style of clothes and different way of speaking caused more disturbance and when they tried to walk straight through, and avoided even looking at the stalls, they really stirred up trouble.

'"What will ye buy?" [they were asked] but they, looking gravely upon him, said, "We buy the truth"'.

After that the mocking and taunting turned to violence and was soon out of control. The steward, in charge of the fair, had them put in the cage but that made matters worse as two groups formed, one fighting for and one against them. Eventually they were locked away to await a hearing in front of Judge Lord Hategood. Following a mockery of a trial, in which evidence was taken from both 'Envy' and 'Superstition', Faithful was stoned and burnt, before the chariot carried him off to heaven.

Elstow had an annual, four day fair, when both vendors and customers came from a great distance. All types of merchandise were sold; there would have been several stalls selling food and drink; numerous jugglers, tricksters and other entertainers strolled around – even the young Bunyan perhaps, a self-confessed troublemaker. Fairs were often rowdy and even if he wasn't present, Bunyan must have heard that in 1645 Royalist soldiers caused a riot during the fair. The landowner's steward and several respected townsmen would have held an on-the-spot court; the constable rounding up thieves and pickpockets and taking them into the 'court'.

The Elstow court was held upstairs, in the Moot Hall, above the stands which the richer merchants hired as their booths. (This hall still stands on the green today and houses a collection of items connected with John Bunyan and a wonderful display of antique furniture.) Fines could be levied but often, to provide a warning to other petty criminals, people were put in the stocks. Those 'cages' which survive in Bedfordshire are mainly small circular buildings just large enough to hold one or two men overnight.

The Hill of Lucre

At last Christian managed to slip away from the prison and found himself crossing a Plain called Ease. He was joined by Hopeful but they found their way blocked by a hill.

Through the centuries the farmers of Pulloxhill must have noticed and talked about the seams of gold powder which they sometimes disturbed when they were working. There was a local, and very disappointing, gold-rush in the 19th century when the mineral was eventually identified as Fools' Gold. *Could Pulloxhill represent The Hill of Lucre?* Christian and Hopeful managed to avoid the dangers of the hill, and to get back onto their proper route, until a choice of paths confused them.

Doubting Castle

They were caught trespassing by Giant Despair, who locked them in his dungeon, starved and beat them and tried to encourage them to commit suicide. They were near despair themselves when Christian remembered that he carried a key, called 'Promise'. They slipped out and returned to the proper path.

By the time that Bunyan was born there were no surviving castles in Bedfordshire. *My choice for Doubting Castle would be The Prison in Silver Street, Bedford,* where Bunyan spent so many frustrating years, but I also offer Totternhoe Castle, see below.

By this time they were getting very near to the end of their journey and were approaching the hills they had seen from the top of the Palace Beautiful.

The Delectable Mountains

No one would want to try and tie Bunyan's Celestial City to one specific place. Heaven, or heaven on earth, are for each of us to find, but *Bunyan's description of his Delectable Mountains* does sound very like *the range of chalk hills that border the south of the county.*

The gardens and orchards of the villages around Dunstable, the woods, parks and vineyards around Luton, the shepherds watching their flocks on the hills, are all very true to life. *The Mountain of Error* with the skeletons of those who had fallen and the tombs at the foot of *Mount Caution* could well be inspired by the steep sides of Totternhoe Knolls and the rough blocks of stone, drying out in the valley below. The path, which the shepherds said led to Doubting Castle, could even suggest that the Knolls themselves, which are the earthworks of a Norman castle, were the inspiration for *Doubting Castle.*

There was 'another place, in a bottom, where was a door in the side of a hill; and they opened the door, and bid them look in . . . 't was very dark and smoky; . . .'

The smoke that they saw and the cries that they heard could well be associated with the Totternhoe stone quarry, deep beneath the castle mound. Totternhoe church, dedicated to St. Giles, the patron saint of cripples, may well represent the suffering connected with the quarry.

★ ★ ★

For over three hundred years, 'The Pilgrim's Progress' has capitvated the hearts, minds and souls of countless people all over the world. As we have seen, hints of the landscape features of the Bedfordshire that Bunyan knew so well are glimpsed throughout the book, but ultimately this immortal work of literature transcends such an analysis. It is in pursuit of an uplifting spiritual journey that Bunyan prophesises, 'this book will make a traveller of thee'.

Bibliography

The standard work of reference for any project involving Bedfordshire is *History of Bedfordshire* by Miss J. Godber, published by Bedfordshire County Council in 1969.

As a county we are particularly lucky to have numerous primary sources published by the 'Bedfordshire Historical Record Society' (BHRS) and the opportunity to follow up a wide range of subjects touched on in this book (e.g. individual landowners, charity schools, the Civil War, persecution of the Quakers) in the volumes of the *Bedfordshire Magazine*. This has now been made much easier by the *Bedfordshire Magazine Index* put together by Yvonne Nicholls and published by White Crescent Press in 1987.

A comprehensive range of books by and about Bunyan is in the Local Studies Collection (01234) 50931 at the Central Library, Bedford.

Volumes of Bedfordshire Historical Record Society Relevant to this Book

Volume 11 (1927) –
'Ecclesiastical Troubles in Dunstable, c.1616', by S. Peyton.
Volume 18 (1936) – Includes
'The Ship-Money Papers of Henry Chester and Sir William Boteler'. F.G. and M. Emmison.
Volume 20 (1938) – Includes
'Jacobean Household Inventories' by F.G. Emmison, and 'Recusancy and Nonconformity in Bedfordshire, Illustrated by Select Documents, 1622–1842', edited by W.M. Wigfield, M.A.
Volume 25 (1947) – Includes
'A Luton Baptist Minute Book, 1707–1806', C.E. Freeman, and 'John Crook, 1617–1699: A Bedfordshire Quaker', by H.G. Tibbutt.

Volume 26 (1949) –
'The Minute Book of the Bedford Corporation, 1647-1664', Guy Parsloe.
Volume 27 (1948) –
'The Life and Letters of Sir Lewis Dyve, 1599-1669', H.G. Tibbutt.
Volume 35 (1955) –
'Colonel John Okey, 1606-1662', H.G. Tibbutt.
Volume 38 (1958) – Includes
'The Tower of London Letter-book of Sir Lewis Dyve, 1646-49', H.G. Tibbutt.
Volume 42 (1962) –
'Calendar of the Civil War Letter Books (1644-45) of Sir Samuel Luke, Parliamentary Governor of Newport Pagnell', H.G. Tibbutt.
Volume 49 (1970) – Includes
'Minutes of the County Sequestration Committee', Patricia Bell.
Volume 51 (1972) –
'Early Nonconformist Church Books', H.G. Tibbutt. (Includes Kensworth, Keysoe, Stevington).
Volume 55 (1976) –
'The Minutes of the First Independent Church (now Bunyan Meeting) at Bedford, 1656-1766', H.G. Tibbutt.
Volume 56 (1977) –
'Bedford Prison 1660-1877', Eric Stockdale.
Volume 59 (1980) – Includes
'The Internal Politics of Bedford 1660-1688', Michael Mullett, and 'Sir John Kelyng, Chief Justice of The King's Bench, 1665-1671, Eric Stockdale.
Volume 65 (1986) –
'Law and Local Society in the time of Charles I', and 'Bedfordshire and the Civil War', both Ross Lee.

Elstow Moot Hall and other Pamphlets Published by Bedfordshire County Council

Each of these excellent, inexpensive booklets gives a compact account of different aspects of the period covered by the life of John Bunyan:

Elstow Moot Hall Guide, Joyce Godber.

Bedfordshire and the First Civil War, with a note on John Bunyan's Military Service, H.G. Tibbutt.
Crime in Bedfordshire, 1660–88, Evelyn Curtis.
Bedfordshire and the Protectorate, H.G. Tibbutt.
John Bunyan of Bedfordshire, Joyce Godber.
Bunyan's Divine Emblems. A Selection of Poems for Children, John Bunyan.

Other Books

There are numerous books covering various aspects of the life and works of John Bunyan. The standard biography is *John Bunyan (1628–1688): His Life, Times and Work,* by the Rev. John Brown, B.A., D.D., Minister of Bunyan Meeting from 1864–1903, revised by Frank Mott-Harrison in 1928.

In The Steps of John Bunyan by Vera Brittain reprinted by Bedfordshire County Council in 1988, follows the life of Bunyan in the context of 17th century Bedfordshire; and *Bunyan of Elstow* by Judith Gunn, Hodder and Stoughton 1985, relates the story of his life in a somewhat simpler style.

John Bunyan: The Man and His Works, by Henri Talon, translated by Barbara Wall 1951, is an invaluable study of the works of John Bunyan; and Roger Sharrock's two books, *John Bunyan* Hutchinson 1954 and *The Pilgrim's Progress: A Casebook* Macmillan 1976, describe both his life and his principal book in a detailed but readable form, assessing Bunyan's writing alongside the other writers and theologians of his day.

In 1978, the 350th anniversary of the birth of John Bunyan and the tercentary of the publication of *The Pilgrim's Progress,* the Bedfordshire Education Service and the School of Humanities of Bedford College of Higher Education arranged for four eminent speakers to each give a lecture, on the subject of John Bunyan in relation to their own specialist subject. These were then published by the Bedfordshire Education Service under the title *John Bunyan 1978.* This book is strongly recommended to any readers wishing to make a study of John Bunyan and his writing. The book includes:
'John Bunyan in English Literature' by Professor Roger Sharrock
'John Bunyan and The English Revolution' by Dr Christopher Hill
'John Bunyan and Bedfordshire' by Patricia Bell

'The Significance of John Bunyan For Today' by Canon Eric James. A book, which thoughtfully and sympathetically examines in detail the life and works of John Bunyan and discusses his message in the light of modern theology, is *Puritan's Progress* by Monica Furlong, Hodder and Stoughton, 1975.

Belief in Bedfordshire by Patricia Bell published by Belfry Press 1986, gives an account of the religious changes which overtook the people of Bedfordshire from the years before the Norman Conquest up until today.

Breakdown of Sources

Chapter I

The material for this chapter comes mainly from John Brown and material drawn from Bedfordshire Parish Registers.

The wills and deeds referred to are in the County Record Office, Bedford.

Chapter 2

The details of individual summons, issued by the officials representing Archbishop Laud and others, can be found in Brown and in 'Law and Local Society in the time of Charles I' by Ross Lee. B.H.R.S. Volume 65 1986.

For the record of Roman Catholics and Nonconformists and the account of the nonconforming people of Dunstable versus Edward Alport see B.H.R.S. above.

For Zachery Symmes and the impropriation of the living of the Priory Church of St Peter, Dunstable see *Activities of the Puritan Faction of the Church of England, 1625-33* by I.M. Calder, S.P.C.K. 1957.

For Zachary Symmes in New England see H.A. Hill, *History of the Old South Church (Third Church) Boston 1669-1884,* Boston 1890 and Cotton Mather, *Magnalia Christi Americana* Bk. III (London 1702).

For John Sydall and the problems at the Church of St Mary the Virgin, Kensworth, see Irving, *History of the English Baptists* Volume II. W. Urwick, *Nonconformity in Hertfordshire,* 1884.

Chapter 3

For information concerning itinerant workers in Bedfordshire at a rather later date see the series of articles by Thomas W. Bagshawe, *Bedfordshire Magazine* Vol. 8.

The brief details of Bunyan's life and education which he noted in his own books are mainly from *Grace Abounding To The Chief of Sinners*, published by George Larkin, London 1666.

The poems quoted are from *A Book for Boys and Girls, – Divine Emblems, or Temporal Things Spiritualized* . . . published by Nathaniel Ponder in 1686.

These poems are a neglected source of information, concerning the character of the country-boy and the young, itinerant worker. A selection has been published as one of the Elstow Moot Hall leaflets, *Bunyan's Divine Emblems*.

Chapter 4

The farm and cottage inventories quoted are from the Bedfordshire County Record Office and are published as B.H.R.S. Volume XX. The inventories of the larger, country houses, sequestered by the Parliamentary Committee are published in B.H.R.S. Vol. LXV.

For details of 17th-century schools and charities, see J. Godber, above.

Chapters 5, 6 and 8

For the unsettled period of Bedfordshire's history and the local incidents of the Civil War see John Brown, Joyce Godber, Ross Lee and the other volumes of B.H.R.S. listed above. For John Bunyan and the Civil War see the reference books listed above. For specific references to local incidents see:

Ampthill, A Goodly Heritage, Andrew Underwood, published by Ampthill Parish Council, 1976.

A Prospect of Ashridge, Douglas Coult, Phillimore, 1980.

The Book of Dunstable and Houghton Regis, Vivienne Evans, Barracuda Books, 1985.

The Story of Leighton Buzzard and Linslade, R.V. Willis, published by the author, 1984.
The Book of Woburn Kenneth G. Spavins and Anne Applin, Barracuda Books, 1983.

Chapter 7

Hudibras, Samuel Butler.
William Dell, Master Puritan, Eric Walker.
Edward Harrison of Petty France, W.T. Whitley. *The Baptist Quarterly* Volume VIII No. 5 January 1935.

For more information concerning the garrison at Newport Pagnell and the Rev. Paul Gibbs, see *A History of Milton Keynes* Volume I, Sir F. Markham.

Chapter 9

For Edward Harrison see Chapter VII and for early Baptists at Hemel Hempstead *History of Hemel Hempstead* edited by Susan Yazley, published by The Charter Trustees of Hemel Hempstead, 1981.

Chapters 10 to 12

Much of the content of these chapters comes from *Grace Abounding* (see above) after consulting John Brown, Henri Talon and the other reference books listed. The order of events, and the interpretation of Bunyan's writing, is my own.
The 'Act Book of the Bedford Meeting' was published as a Facsimile Edition in 1928, with an introduction by G.B. Harrison. It contains a brief account of John Gifford's adventures as a Royalist officer before coming to Bedford.

Chapters 13 to 15

A detailed account of Bunyan's arrest at Harlington, his

imprisonment, trial and the attempts of his wife Elizabeth to gain him a pardon are included in his book, *A Relation of the Imprisonment of Mr John Bunyan* which was not printed until seventy-seven years after his death. (1765)

Chapter 16

The persecution of the Independent churches following the Coronation of Charles II is set out in the books of John Brown and Vera Brittain and commented on in most of the reference books above.

Chapters 17 and 18

Bunyan's eventual freedom, his role as pastor, adviser and friend; the writing and the publication of his later books are all described in and commented on, as above.

Works of John Bunyan

I have quoted from John Bunyan's Pamphlets:

A Defence of the Doctrine of Justification by Faith in Jesus Christ.
Differences in Judgement about Water – Baptism No Bar To Communion.
Come and Welcome To Jesus Christ.
A Treatise of the Fear of God.

and his books:

The Pilgrim's Progress Part I, published originally by Nathaniel Ponder, London 1678 but Mr By-Ends does not appear until a later edition.
The Pilgrim's Progress Part II, Nathaniel Ponder, 1685.
The Life and Death of Mr Badman, Nathaniel Ponder, 1680.
The Holy War, Dorman Newman, London 1682.
A Book For Boys and Girls, Nathaniel Ponder, London 1686.
A Relationship of the Imprisonment of Mr John Bunyan, which was not published until 1765.

Index

Numbers in italics refer to illustration

Books Published by THE BOOK CASTLE

JOURNEYS INTO BEDFORDSHIRE: Anthony Mackay.
Foreword by The Marquess of Tavistock, Woburn Abbey. A lavish book of over 150 evocative ink drawings.

LEAFING THROUGH LITERATURE:
Writers' Lives in Hertfordshire and Bedfordshire: David Carroll.
Illustrated short biographies of many famous authors and their connections with these counties.

THROUGH VISITORS' EYES: A Bedfordshire Anthology:
edited by Simon Houfe.
Impressions of the county by famous visitors over the last four centuries, thematically arranged and illustrated with line drawings.

**THE HILL OF THE MARTYR: An Architectural History of
St. Albans Abbey:** Eileen Roberts.
Scholarly and readable chronological narrative history of Hertfordshire and Bedfordshire's famous cathedral. Fully illustrated with photographs and plans.

**FOLK: Characters and Events in the History of Bedfordshire
and Northamptonshire:** Vivienne Evans.
Anthology about people of yesteryear – arranged alphabetically by village or town.

LEGACIES: Tales and Legends of Luton and the North Chilterns:
Vic Lea. Twenty-five mysteries and stories based on fact, including Luton Town Football Club. Many photographs.

ECHOES: Tales And Legends of Bedfordshire and Hertfordshire:
Vic Lea. Thirty, compulsively retold historical incidents.

ECCENTRICS and VILLAINS, HAUNTINGS and HEROES.
Tales from Four Shires: Northants., Beds., Bucks. and Herts.:
John Houghton.
True incidents and curious events covering one thousand years.

THE RAILWAY AGE IN BEDFORDSHIRE: Fred Cockman.
Classic, illustrated account of early railway history.

FARM OF MY CHILDHOOD, 1925–1947: Mary Roberts.
An almost vanished lifestyle on a remote farm near Flitwick.

DUNSTABLE WITH THE PRIORY, 1100–1550: Vivienne Evans.
Dramatic growth of Henry I's important new town around a major crossroads.

**BEDFORDSHIRE'S YESTERYEARS Vol. 1: The Family,
Childhood and Schooldays:** Brenda Fraser-Newstead.
Unusual early 20th century reminiscences, with private photographs.

BEDFORDSHIRE'S YESTERYEARS Vol 2: The Rural Scene:
Brenda Fraser-Newstead.
Vivid first-hand accounts of country life two or three generations ago.

Further titles are in preparation. All the above are available via any bookshop, or from the publisher and bookseller
THE BOOK CASTLE
12 Church Street, Dunstable, Bedfordshire, LU5 4RU Tel: (01582) 605670